D0906638

High
Yield
Debt

High
Yield
Debt

*An Insider's Guide
to the Marketplace*

RAJAY BAGARIA

WILEY

This edition first published 2016
© 2016 Rajay Bagaria

Registered office
John Wiley & Sons Ltd, The Atrium, Southern Gate, Chichester, West Sussex, PO19 8SQ, United Kingdom

For details of our global editorial offices, for customer services and for information about how to apply for permission to reuse the copyright material in this book please see our website at www.wiley.com.

Wiley publishes in a variety of print and electronic formats and by print-on-demand. Some material included with standard print versions of this book may not be included in e-books or in print-on-demand. If this book refers to media such as a CD or DVD that is not included in the version you purchased, you may download this material at http://booksupport.wiley.com. For more information about Wiley products, visit www.wiley.com.

Designations used by companies to distinguish their products are often claimed as trademarks. All brand names and product names used in this book are trade names, service marks, trademarks or registered trademarks of their respective owners. The publisher is not associated with any product or vendor mentioned in this book.

Limit of Liability/Disclaimer of Warranty: While the publisher and author have used their best efforts in preparing this book, they make no representations or warranties with respect to the accuracy or completeness of the contents of this book and specifically disclaim any implied warranties of merchantability or fitness for a particular purpose. It is sold on the understanding that the publisher is not engaged in rendering professional services and neither the publisher nor the author shall be liable for damages arising herefrom. If professional advice or other expert assistance is required, the services of a competent professional should be sought.

Library of Congress Cataloging-in-Publication Data

Names: Bagaria, Rajay, 1977– author.
Title: High yield debt : an insider's guide to the marketplace / Rajay
  Bagaria.
Description: Hoboken : Wiley, 2016. | Includes index.
Identifiers: 9781119134411 (hardback)
Subjects: LCSH: Junk bonds. | Capital market. | Business cycles. | BISAC:
  BUSINESS & ECONOMICS / Banks & Banking.
Classification: LCC HG4651 .B294 2016 (print)
LC record available at http://lccn.loc.gov/2015042482

A catalogue record for this book is available from the British Library.

ISBN 978-1-119-13441-1 (hbk) ISBN 978-1-119-13443-5 (ebk)
ISBN 978-1-119-13442-8 (ebk) ISBN 978-1-119-23695-5 (ebk)

Cover Design: Wiley
Cover Images: Egg Image: © Excentro/Shutterstock
Unicycler Image: © ra2studio/Shutterstock

Set in 11/13pt Times by Aptara Inc., New Delhi, India
Printed in Great Britain by TJ International Ltd, Padstow, Cornwall, UK

Contents

Preface

Today's U.S. corporate high yield market is worth over $2.5 trillion. That's more than the stock market capitalization of most countries including Germany, France, and Canada. Over 350 funds provide exposure to U.S. high yield including mutual funds, ETFs, and closed-end funds. In addition, a growing number of alternative funds such as distressed debt, mezzanine finance, and credit hedge funds also generate returns from high yield debt. High yield debt has never before been so accessible to both institutional and individual investors around the globe.

The attraction to high yield stems from its high risk-adjusted returns over time. High yield can be broken down into two market segments: high yield bonds and leveraged loans. Over the past 20 years, high yield bonds have produced high single-digit total returns comparable to the S&P 500 with less than half the annualized volatility.[1] Leveraged loans have posted mid-single-digit returns with lower volatility than bonds and only one negative total return year in two decades.[2] This performance is why pension funds, endowments, insurance companies, institutions, and retirees increasingly buy high yield as a source of current income and complement to dividend paying stocks.

Yet, despite its size and significance, high yield is an often misunderstood asset class. It's a market that is primarily traded over-the-counter and lacks transparency. It has also grown in complexity since its early "junk bond" days. What market professionals come to learn is that not all high yield exposure is the same: specific market segments and fund types can produce meaningfully different results over the same time period.

---

[1] Credit Suisse.
[2] Ibid.

Developing a more informed view of the market is what can lead to a performance advantage.

Working at leading investment firms has provided me with a front row seat to the latest developments in the high yield market during its most transformative period of growth. My first job out of college was in the investment banking program at J.P. Morgan & Co. I joined their high yield group at a time when the firm was pioneering the use of credit default swaps, a trillion dollar industry today. I later joined Goldman Sachs & Co., where I worked on a multi-billion dollar mezzanine fund that was a pioneer in making large-sized privately structured high yield debt investments. Following Goldman Sachs, I spent eight years at Apollo Investment Management where I was a Partner and Investment Committee member responsible for investments in all types of high yield debt through a business development company. More recently, I established a credit hedge fund with the backing of a prominent family office. This fund is engaged in both long and short investment strategies related to high yield bonds and loans and is a top performing high yield fund at the time of writing.[3]

In my career, which spans nearly two decades and two recessions, I have been fortunate to learn from some of the smartest people in the business. I have worked with teams to invest billions of dollars in high yield issuers. I've seen periods of economic growth and decline, high and low volatility, and have restructured companies that failed to perform. This experience has afforded me with numerous insights on the high yield market which I share in this book.

The decision to write *High Yield Debt: An Insider's Guide to the Marketplace* was made almost two years ago. While fundraising, I met with many individuals responsible for high yield investments who had surprisingly little understanding of the market. Rather than go through my pitch, I would take these groups through a primer I developed, addressing everything from the high yield market's evolution to tracking the health of issuers and value in spreads. Seeing the knowledge gaps even at the Chief Investment Officer level made me realize that there is a broad-based

---

[3]eVestment. Performance data (net of fees and expenses) from May 2013 to June 2015 represents a sample of 181 funds that reported their performance and fund information to eVestment as of September 14, 2015. WDO ranked #1 since its inception based on this data.

need for better information on the high yield market. Put another way, if the people managing large investment funds have difficulty understanding high yield, what does that mean for everyone else?

There is surprisingly little literature on the high yield market despite its market size and importance to the economy. In the early 1990s, several books on high yield were released that provided information on junk bonds but the market was very different then. It was one one-tenth its current size with less complexity and it did not include a large, traded leveraged loan market as it does today. Recent books on high yield are more specialized and written for the analyst seeking job skills or the fund manager contemplating more advanced topics related to risk management. What is missing is a book for everyone else – which actually encompasses most market participants.

Within the high yield industry, comparatively few people partake at the level of making buy-sell decisions on individual debt instruments. This is because high yield bonds and loans are difficult to transact in small quantities. Most wealth allocators are engaged at a level where they are deciding whether to buy into a high yield fund and, if so, which one? Other professionals, like market analysts and bankers, provide services related to the industry and are seeking a better understanding of the bigger picture. Participants like private equity firms, lawyers, and issuers need to know the financial and legal terms of high yield debt. Business school students and analysts in training programs can gain an advantage with interviews and a head start on the job with a more informed perspective of high yield capital markets and investment banking.

My goal in writing *High Yield Debt: An Insider's Guide to the Marketplace* is to explain the U.S. corporate high yield market in basic terms and as concisely as possible. This book will address how the market has evolved, who buys and issues high yield, high yield debt structures, asset class performance, and how to track and evaluate the market for investment opportunities in a variety of different funds. In writing this book, I make no assumptions about the audience's knowledge level; I assume that most industry jargon is confusing and requires explanation and I get into a fairly deep level of insight and analysis such that even experienced market professionals will find something new and interesting. I also seek to explain the most frequently asked questions I've received on high yield. Last, I include what I consider the most important historical market data so that this book can be referred back to over time on any areas of interest.

BEFORE YOU BEGIN

This book can be read either cover to cover, or consulted when topics of interest surface. The Contents outlines the book's progression. It lists key topics of common interest for easy reference. Many of these topics are questions I have been asked during investor meetings. Any potentially confusing terms are italicized and included in the Glossary. Each chapter contains an introduction and summary with key insights, which is relevant to subsequent chapters. While this can be kept as a reference book, I recommend at least skimming chapter summaries from start to finish to gain a better sense of the book's contents.

Chapter 1 starts with an introduction to high yield, beginning with a basic definition of high yield debt and progressing to how the high yield industry evolved from a market for fallen angles to a thriving $2.5 trillion industry. Chapter 2 delves into the issuers of high yield – explaining why they raise high yield debt, the decisions they face, and the capital-raising process with investment banks. Chapter 3 then addresses buying high yield, and provides insight on important differences in the buyer base and financing for high yield bonds and leveraged loans. I also address the implications of high yield being an over-the-counter market and trends with liquidity, a common concern. Chapter 4 addresses financial concepts and economic terms important to understanding high yield debt, which is vital to assessing and tracking the market.

Chapters 5 and 6 round out the foundational knowledge required to form a view on high investment opportunities. Chapter 5 addresses high yield debt structures and how these differ for high yield bonds and leveraged loans. Understanding what constitutes aggressive versus less aggressive debt structures also provides a means to track developing trends in the marketplace. Chapter 6 provides an overview of high yield credit agreements, a more technical topic, and also discusses other legal considerations such as recent regulatory developments, which are topics particularly important to credit investors, high yield issuers, and corporate lawyers. The purpose of Chapter 6 is to explain what protections exist in high yield credit agreements and clarify the meanings of certain industry jargon that is often used but frequently misunderstood.

After establishing a framework for understanding the high yield industry and the differences between its two key market segments – high yield bonds and leveraged loans – Chapter 7 gets into a topic of great interest: asset class performance. Chapter 7 addresses many frequently asked questions on high yield performance such as total returns, volatility, interest rate risk, defaults, and recovery. Building on this foundation, Chapter 8 provides a few tools and metrics that can be used to assess the market opportunity at a given time. This evaluation method includes incorporating a view of corporate spreads with industry fundamentals to provide a sense of the risk-reward for both leveraged loans and bonds. I also provide a list of the information sources used by high yield investors to make more informed decisions. Armed with this knowledge, the reader is better able to form and express a view on the various investment options, which for most investors are funds rather than individual debt instruments.

Chapter 9 describes the different "public" or 1940 Act funds that provide high yield exposure such as mutual funds, closed-end funds, ETFs, and BDCs. The different 1940 Act Funds have pros and cons which also vary depending on the type of exposure sought. I explain the primary considerations related to each of these fund options and discuss their performance over different periods of time. Chapter 10 addresses "private" or alternative funds that provide high yield exposure such as mezzanine funds, credit hedge funds, and distressed funds. Private funds are generally only available to larger investors that meet certain income and net worth requirements. These types of funds have higher fee structures but can outperform in certain market environments primarily through the use of fund leverage, active investment strategies, and greater portfolio concentration. Understanding the conditions under which these funds can thrive can be helpful when choosing which one to pursue.

CONTACT

I am grateful for your interest in this book and would welcome any questions or comments you have. Please feel to reach me at rajaybagaria@hydebt.com or visit the website www.hydebt.com for more information.

DISCLAIMER

The concepts and ideas in this book are my own and other professionals may disagree with my conclusions. There are risks involved with investing, including the possible loss of capital. Investors should consider the

investment objectives, risks, charges, and expenses of the fund(s) carefully before investing. Please seek the counsel of your accountant for any
tax-related matters as there is no tax guidance presented in this book.

Acknowledgments

Although this book lists me as the author, it was shaped by the contributions of many friends and colleagues. First, I would like to thank Sean O'Keefe, my research assistant. Sean scrutinized every draft, created insightful charts and analyses, and tracked down permissions. I couldn't imagine finishing this book without his tremendous effort. I would also like to thank all my colleagues at Wasserstein & Co., who have been generous with their time. Ellis Jones, Chairman of Wasserstein & Co., is one of the kindest and most thoughtful investors I've met in my career. Ellis offered several insights based on his experience that helped improve the book's contents. My team at Wasserstein Debt Opportunities, especially Alex Kelsey and Beth Gardiner, also reviewed and helped improve drafts. I am grateful for their support.

Over the years, I've worked with some bright professionals who took an interest in my growth. At Goldman Sachs, Melina Higgins was a mentor and gave me numerous opportunities to learn about high yield. At Apollo Management, my friend and colleague Bruce Spector taught me about restructurings while working together on difficult situations. I feel lucky to have had such good teachers including my cousin Anup Bagaria and my friend and legal advisor Emil Buchman. Anup, a Co-Managing Partner of Wasserstein & Co., has been my biggest supporter and played a role in almost every step of my career. I could not have come this far without him. Emil, a corporate law partner at Fried Frank, taught me everything I know about high yield legal considerations. We have been working on deals together since 2000. Emil is a meaningful contributor to this book.

There are several people I would like to thank for their time. Barry Delman, a Managing Director from Bank of Nova Scotia, offered numerous insights on total return swaps, an obscure area of the market. Jessica Forbes, a corporate law partner from Fried Frank, reviewed and thoughtfully commented on Chapters 9 and 10. Marc Auerbach from S&P Capital

IQ LCD helped provide much of the data used throughout this book to elucidate concepts. Ed Boll and Bill Visconto provided valuable insights on asset class performance. My writer friends, Peter Stevenson and Sarah Dunn, were also helpful advisors to this first-time author. I miss our days commuting and writing on the train together. My other friends, including Tracey Bernstein, Alex Tripp, Elliott Sumers, Scott Jarrell and Maria Stein-Marrison, have patiently listened to more about high yield than they ever cared to know. Although we decided against calling this book "Junkanomics," I am nonetheless grateful for Radley Horton's creativity and friendship. I am also grateful for my brother, Sanjay, and my parents, Om and Chandra, for providing me with love and encouragement to pursue life to its fullest. Last, I want to thank my editor, Thomas Hyrkiel, and the team at Wiley, for their many contributions.

My deepest gratitude is to my wife, Rajni, and our children, Arjun and Amalie. My family encouraged me to pursue this idea despite its cost to them. I am forever grateful for their love and support. Rajni filled all the gaps in our household I created and patiently reviewed drafts of chapters, offering thoughtful feedback along the way. She is one of the smartest and most fun people I know. I could not imagine my life without her and our amazing kids, who in their natural way inspire me to be a better person. For that, I dedicate this book to my family.

About the Author

Rajay Bagaria has nearly two decades of experience in the high yield market. He currently serves as the President and Chief Investment Officer of Wasserstein Debt Opportunities Management, LP ("WDO") a credit hedge fund he established in 2013 with backing from a prominent family office. From WDO's inception to June 2015, WDO was a top ranking high yield fund based on data from eVestment.[4]

Prior to founding WDO, Mr. Bagaria was a Partner and Investment Committee member of Apollo Investment Management ("Apollo"), the investment manager of Apollo Investment Corporation ("AIC"), a publicly traded business development company with over $3 billion of assets under management (AUM). At Apollo, Mr. Bagaria invested in several asset classes including senior debt, high yield bonds, mezzanine debt, and equity. He also held responsibilities related to secondary trading, investment team development, portfolio company work-outs, and the development of Apollo's energy lending and aviation investment platforms. Mr. Bagaria has been a board member of several companies including LVI Services, Inc. Generation Brands, and Playpower, Inc.

Prior to joining Apollo, Mr. Bagaria worked as an investor for Goldman Sachs & Co.'s PIA Mezzanine Fund, the largest mezzanine debt fund globally, and as a high yield investment banker at J.P. Morgan & Co. Mr. Bagaria earned a BA degree at New York University with studies at the London School of Economics.

Mr. Bagaria is co-founder of The Manitou School, a private elementary school located in Cold Spring, New York. He lives in Garrison, New York with his wife and two children.

---

[4]eVestment. Performance data (net of fees and expenses) from May 2013 to June 2015 represents a sample of 181 funds that reported their performance and fund information to eVestment as of September 14th, 2015. WDO ranked #1 on return since its inception based on this data.

Foreword

When, about a year ago, Rajay told me that he wanted to write a book about high yield investing, my reaction was two-fold. On the one hand, time commitment required to write a book, while managing a successful hedge fund, seemed to present a daunting challenge. On the other hand, after 20 years of practicing corporate law and handling a wide variety of leverage finance transactions, I understood that this book was long overdue. Having had to explain the very basics of high yield instruments over and over again in each transaction, I could understand how frustrating it could be to try and overcome common misconceptions, lack of knowledge, and suspicious attitudes.

As friends and colleagues who were involved in leverage finance for many years (Rajay, on the business side and me on the legal side), both of us knew well that the high yield market was largely misunderstood. The excesses of the late 1980s and early 1990s, which resulted in prominent criminal prosecutions, as well as a commonly-held notion of high volatility and high default rates of high yield instruments, gave the high yield market a bad reputation, the reputation that we knew was undeserved. Through a thorough overview of the fundamentals of high yield instruments, filled with facts and unbiased analysis, *High Yield Debt: An Insider's Guide to the Marketplace* debunks these myths of excessive volatility and the inherent danger of high yield market.

Indeed, who could have been better suited to demystify high yield investing than Rajay, who started his investment career at Goldman Sachs, continued it as one of the principals at Apollo Investment Corporation, a publicly traded business development company specializing in high and mezzanine investments, and finally ended up starting his own high yield investment fund that has been steadily generating returns far in excess of market average. And Rajay did it!

High Yield Debt: An Insider's Guide to the Marketplace unravels the mystery of the high yield market chapter by chapter. To put the topic in perspective, the book starts with a historical background (which to me was also a fun part to read as it brought back memories of the days past). It then describes market participants, explains the economics of high yield instruments, and touches upon prevalent debt structures and pertinent legal requirements. The book then moves to demonstrate high performance levels of high yield instruments making them attractive additions to an investment portfolio. The book concludes by addressing some of the more specialized concepts, such as mezzanine investments, distressed debt, and credit hedge funds. An extensive use of charts and statistics lends *High Yield Debt: An Insider's Guide to the Marketplace* a necessary credibility. Yet, the book is lively written, to keep the reader entertained, while educated.

To be sure, there have been books written about high yield investing before. However, those books addressed primarily the academia and were written in a much more scholarly fashion. I could not imagine any of those books being a desktop set or a day-to-day reference guide. *High Yield Debt: An Insider's Guide to the Marketplace*, on the other hand, is designed to address the needs of market participants, be it an investment manager in a family office, a young lawyer starting his or her career at a corporate law firm, or a rookie investment banker pitching a new instrument to a corporate client. This is a book that could be quickly referenced to conceptualize an investment thesis for a particular instrument or to understand a market lingo used by more seasoned professionals (for which the Glossary at the end of the book can hardly be praised enough). I would also recommend this book to CFOs of companies that are looking for efficient capital-raising techniques. Overall, the key attraction of this book is its versatility, clarity and scope, all of which could come in handy in many different situations.

Now, more than a year after the idea of the book was first conceived by Rajay, I am still awed by the sheer amount of effort that went into its writing. Yet, I am impressed even more by the quality, breadth and depth of the final product of this monumental effort, the product that deservedly occupies a prominent place on my desk. I am confident that readers will find *High Yield Debt: An Insider's Guide to the Marketplace* to be an invaluable treasure trove of information about high yield markets. I am very proud to take a small part in the exciting journey that the writing of this book turned out to be. It gives me a great pleasure to congratulate Rajay on the successful completion of his valiant efforts in writing this book and encourage him to embark on new, no less ambitious ventures.

Emil Buchman
Corporate Partner
Fried, Frank, Harris, Shriver & Jacobson LLP

CHAPTER 1

Development of the High Yield Industry

C hapter 1 lays the groundwork necessary for understanding the U.S. corporate high yield asset class. It starts by explaining what high yield debt is and how it compares to investment grade debt, the two broad fixed income categories. The chapter then covers the importance of credit ratings before providing a short history on how the modern day, high yield market evolved. This history tells a story of market growth that was not always sound, epitomized by the early 1990s "junk bond" bubble. However, the high yield industry has grown from its experiences. Improved underwriting standards, regulatory scrutiny, and greater investor protections ultimately fostered more sustainable growth manifest in today's $2.5 trillion market. To note, terms that might be confusing or are industry jargon are highlighted in italics and included in the Glossary.

1.1 WHAT IS HIGH YIELD DEBT?

High yield debt, often referred to simply as *high yield,* is debt rated *below investment grade* by major rating agencies such as Moody's Investor Services, Standard & Poor's (S&P), or Fitch Ratings. The highest rated debt is labeled *investment grade* by the rating agencies and has low risk of default or loss. This ratings category includes U.S. government bonds and the debt of large public companies such as General Electric, Microsoft, and ExxonMobil. Rating agencies label debt with below BBB-/Baa3 ratings as *below investment grade* or *speculative grade,* which constitute the high

1

yield market. As the name "high yield" suggests, this category of debt provides a high rate of return to compensate for greater credit risk, or the possibility that the debt does not get repaid in full.

Leo Tolstoy's famous observation that "happy families are all alike; every unhappy family is unhappy in its own way" aptly describes the differences between investment grade and below investment grade borrowers as well. Investment grade borrowers are like happy families, enjoying access to the capital markets at attractive rates. For example, Apple (Aa1/AA+ rated) raised $5.5 billion in 2013 of 10-year debt at 2.4%, a rate similar to what the U.S. government pays. The risk of default for investment grade issuers is considered negligible; therefore, the borrowing rates are similar and more affected by the *yield curve* – or interest rates of government debt with different maturities – which serves as a benchmark for all debt. Though the prospects for investment grade companies' stock differs, their debt is generally well insulated from growth-related risks. In this way, the "happy families" are all alike.

High yield borrowers are more like unhappy families borrowing at expensive rates, each for its own reason. The high yield issuer base is broad; it includes countries, municipalities and corporations such as Costa Rica, Detroit and Sprint. Each high yield issuer has unique challenges and opportunities. Unlike investment grade companies, growth prospects matter more because these entities are more heavily indebted. As Moody's and S&P ratings migrate to lower categories such as Caa1/CCC+, the potential for default and loss amplifies. What binds high yield issuers into one asset class is simply a rating designation: below investment grade. But high yield issuers, unlike investment grade companies, carry more idiosyncratic risks, similar to stocks, and must pay higher interest rates on their debt as a result. In Tolstoy's words – and the debt markets – high yield issuers are the unhappy families, with each being unhappy in its own way.

Table 1.1 details the highest to lowest ratings provided by Moody's and S&P. Though each rating agency uses a different methodology to estimate and categorize credit risk, they produce comparable metrics. For example, a Baa2 rating by Moody's is similar to a BBB rating by S&P. This is shown below. The notching can also be viewed comparably, where a "1" from Moody's is similar to a "+" from S&P. Notching provides an added degree of segmentation which shows how close an issuer is to the next ratings tier.

Regarding the ratings chart, it's interesting to note that high yield is a somewhat arbitrary designation. The ratings agencies don't provide clear guidance on why BBB-/Baa3 serves as the demarcation line between

TABLE 1.1   Moody's and S&P Ratings Categories

Credit Risk	Moody's Rating	S&P Rating
Investment Grade		
Highest Quality	Aaa	AAA
High Quality	Aa1/Aa2/Aa3	AA+/AA/AA−
Upper Medium Grade	A1/A2/A3	A+/A/A−
Medium Grade	Baa1/Baa2/Baa3	BBB+/BBB/BBB−
Below Investment Grade		
Lower Medium Grade	Ba1/Ba2/Ba3	BB+/BB/BB−
Low Grade	B1/B2/B3	B+/B/B−
Poor Quality	Caa1/Caa2/Caa3	CCC+/CCC/CCC−
Most Speculative	Ca	CC
No interest being paid or bankruptcy petition filed	C	C
In Default	C	D

what they consider investment grade and below investment grade. The decision, however, made many decades ago, now broadly classifies the entire fixed income market, which in the United States is estimated at over $40 trillion.[1] Today, any outstanding debt obligation – whether it is issued by a company, country, municipality, or even a structured finance vehicle – can be considered investment grade or below investment grade risk.

1.2   THE IMPORTANCE OF CREDIT RATINGS

Credit ratings are important to high yield investors and issuers for a few reasons. First, high yield debt investors generally require issuers to obtain credit ratings from two agencies on any debt offering. Although investors rely on their own business's *due diligence* – or evaluation of the issuer – when making investment decisions, the ratings still have an impact on the investment decision. This is because many high yield investors have

---

[1]Credit Suisse, SIFMA.

investment mandates shaped by ratings. For example, a certain type of loan investor may only be able to buy a limited number of CCC rated credits, irrespective of what they think of the risk-return. Also, many buyers utilize lower cost borrowings to make investments and seek to profit from the spread. Ratings can affect the amount of financing available or regulatory capital that must be set aside for high yield investments. If a lower rating makes a debt issue more expensive to purchase with financing, investors seek compensation for this cost through a higher interest rate or yield to make the investment sufficiently profitable. It therefore goes without saying that lower ratings result in higher interest costs to issuers.

But the two broad ratings categories – investment grade or below investment grade – when taken literally are actually misleading. Rating agencies in fact have no interest in opining on whether a debt obligation is investment-worthy or not. Rather, the ratings of an issuer or its debt instrument serve only as a third-party assessment of the creditworthiness of the issuer and its ability to meet its debt obligations as they come due. Whether one chooses to buy or sell a debt instrument depends less on whether it is deemed investment or below investment grade and more on whether the price and yield compensate for the risk of loss. Further, credit rating agencies' estimates sometimes bear little relationship to reality. In 2008 for example, the rating agencies grossly underestimated the risks of numerous credit investments that had sub-prime mortgage exposure. Even though the rating agencies are not perfect, they still play an important role in the fixed income industry by constituting a third-party assessment of risk. Ratings can be relied upon for their independence and absence of conflict.

Something to keep in mind is that ratings can be upgraded or downgraded, which means they can change over time with credit developments and periodic ratings review by credit rating agencies. Some high yield issuers eventually have debt that is upgraded to investment grade. When ratings are downgraded from investment grade to below investment grade as they were for Ford and GM in 2005, it causes a turnover in the investor base. Initial investors who prefer, or can only hold, higher quality investment grade issues sell their positions, usually at a loss. New investors, with different investment mandates or who believe the return potential at a lower purchase price now compensates for the risk, step in. Trading in the debt of these types of issues is exactly how the modern high yield market got its start.

1.3 THE ORIGINS OF HIGH YIELD

Strictly speaking, the high yield market took shape in the early 1900s when major rating agencies began providing ratings on government, municipal, and corporate debt. After all, high yield – as it's defined – can only exist with ratings. In practice, however, speculative grade debt existed well before the rating agencies. It was used to finance important modern world developments such as early sea exploration, railroads, banks, and steel companies. Even the United States borrowed heavily from the Netherlands and France in the 1780s shortly after its founding in a way similar to emerging market countries borrowing from the developed countries of today. The potential risks of lending to a newly formed country made this debt akin to what we now consider speculative grade debt.

Speculative grade debt is a natural component of the capital markets system. Similar to how a happy family might become unhappy (e.g., Mom loses her job, Dad becomes ill), creditworthy issuers sometimes hit hard times; and the unthinkable happens – an issuer loses its investment grade rating. During the Great Depression, for example, many investment grade issuers had their debt downgraded to speculative grade status as their financial health and prospects deteriorated.

But the nature of high yield debt has changed in the past four decades. Up until the 1970s, the high yield universe consisted mostly of companies whose debt had been downgraded to below investment grade ratings or so-called *fallen angels*. Fallen angels include retailers like JCPenney who once prospered and raised investment grade debt to facilitate rapid expansion. As the prospects of these businesses changed and their performance declined, their debt was downgraded, eventually to high yield or "junk" status. When investment grade debt becomes high yield, it carries a low interest rate but trades at a steep price discount. An example would be a 3% bond trading at a price of 70%. What this means is that an investor can buy a $1,000 bond for $700. The $300 discount provides additional compensation, or yield, to account for the higher risk of loss that now exists. For example, if this 3% bond had five years remaining and was paid in full at maturity, it would offer an 11% yield. This yield can be computed using an internal rate of return calculation assuming an initial cash outflow of $700 followed by $30 per annum of interest income (3% of $1,000) for five years and then $1,000 of principal return at maturity (in year five).

The modern high yield market obtained its start through the trading of fallen angel debt. One investment banker largely credited for developing this market is Michael Milken. Working for the investment bank Drexel Burnham Lambert, Milken was an early advocate of speculative grade bonds. Drawing from the research of Braddock Hickman, an economist and former Federal Reserve Bank president who published studies on the performance of debt of varying quality, Milken believed that the yields of fallen angel debt often over-compensated for the risk of default loss and that this less understood category of debt provided attractive opportunities for investment. Milken's success in cultivating demand for high yield bonds ultimately opened a primary market for an entirely new type of high yield issuer, one that was deliberately high yield rather than the result of a downgrade.

A *primary market* refers to the market for new issues and stands in contrast to the *secondary market,* or market for existing debt. The significance of a high yield primary market was that the issuers were not only composed of fallen angels. They included companies that made a corporate finance decision to raise significant quantities of debt with full knowledge that doing so would result in their debt being classified as high yield. To provide some context, these companies might willingly issue debt with an 11% interest rate. The issuers that sought to do this were not necessarily companies that longed for their best days; they included companies that were more entrepreneurial with growth prospects that high yield capital might unlock.

Early issuers of high yield included Texas International, an energy company engaged in exploration and development whose story is documented in the book by Harlan Platt, *The First Junk Bond.*[2] It also included companies like McCaw Cellular and Viacom, which had tremendous growth opportunities that were capital intensive to fund. High yield debt provided a means of financing this growth, often led by innovative entrepreneurs who built large successful enterprises. Some of these companies, like Viacom, eventually became investment grade, as their investments paid off. Others, like McCaw Cellular, were sold to strategic or financial buyers in successful transactions.

In opening a primary market for speculative grade issuers, Drexel laid the groundwork for a high yield market that would have profound implications for companies, municipalities, and countries. For corporations who

---

[2]Platt, Harlan. *The First Junk Bond: A Story of Corporate Boom and Bust.* Beard Books, 2002.

previously either maximized low-cost borrowings or financed operations with high-cost equity, high yield provided a third option, a source of capital between bank or bond borrowings and equity. Although equity capital does not have a stated cost like debt does, the cost of equity is the expected return it provides. For example, many investors expect to generate 10–20% returns on equity over time. Therefore, high yield, which usually carries a 4–12% rate, could present an attractive option relative to equity. As an added benefit, interest on the debt is for the most part tax-deductible and thereby lowers the effective cost of borrowings for taxpaying issuers.

1.4 ADVENT OF THE LEVERAGED BUYOUT

The *leveraged buyout* or *LBO* is an outgrowth of the high yield market that emerged in the 1980s and an industry that has experienced tremendous growth over the years. A leveraged buyout is simply what the name implies: a buyout – or acquisition of a controlling interest in a company – facilitated primarily with *leverage*, which is another word for debt. Today, LBOs are a major driver of high yield activity. Debt is raised almost daily to fund buyouts and refinance existing debt. This type of transaction is often employed by *private equity firms* who seek to put down as little money as reasonable to gain control. Private equity firms manage pools of investment capital allocated toward equity investments in companies that provide ownership control. In contrast to public equity, or stock listed on a national exchange, private equity investments do not trade in the market.

The premise of an LBO is to maximize high yield debt borrowings to finance an acquisition. By doing this, a private equity firm minimizes its equity investment while retaining all the benefits of growth. This happens because debt borrowings only obtain a fixed rate of return – principal and interest – while the equity retains all residual enterprise value. For example, if a business bought for $100 million and financed with $80 million of debt and $20 million of equity is ultimately sold for $200 million, the debt only receives $80 million plus its rate of interest. The equity benefits from all residual value and therefore can receive a return amounting to multiples of its initial investment.

Henry Kravis, Jerome Kohlberg, Jr. and George Roberts are among the most famous individuals involved in pioneering the LBO industry. Experimenting with buyouts in the 1960s while working at Bear Stearns, their acquisition targets included companies that lacked a good exit option – either being too small for an IPO or perhaps founder-owned and unwilling to sell to a competitor. After buying a number of companies, the three executives left Bear Stearns and established Kohlberg Kravis Roberts (KKR) in 1976, one of the largest alternative asset managers today. Similar to the experience Bill Gates and Paul Allen had at Lakeside, a Seattle school with its own computer at the brink of the personal computing revolution, the founders of KKR spent their formative years pioneering leveraged buyouts at the moment the industry was set to take-off with the innovations taking place in high yield finance.

By the late 1970s, leveraged buyouts were taking place more frequently and were not just carried out by entrepreneurs who sought to buy and improve businesses but also by more controversial *corporate raiders*, or individuals who sought to create value through more hostile tactics. This group included Carl Icahn, Victor Posner, Nelson Peltz, Robert M. Bass, T. Boone Pickens and Kirk Kerkorian among many others whose rise and actions are well chronicled in the book, *The Predator's Ball*,[3] released in 1989. Corporate raiders look for undervalued assets. They then seek to take control or exert influence over the company by buying shares. By changing management, divesting assets or implementing more shareholder friendly policies, corporate raiders can make huge sums of profit in a short time period. Many public officials, including Paul Volker, chairman of the Federal Reserve Bank, were outspoken critics of the transactions these individuals proposed and even sought legislation to limit the use of high yield finance to support "greenmail," a transaction in which capital is raised to purchase shares owned by corporate raiders.

As a relatively new industry, high yield was initially viewed skeptically by many in part due to the reputation of its proponents. But, despite criticism leveled at it, the LBO and high yield industry thrived. From 1978 to 1989, over 2,000 leveraged buyouts were consummated.[4] According to research by Edward Altman, the annual high yield default rate over this time period averaged 2.1% – a rate actually lower than average default

---

[3]Bruck, Connie. *The Predator's Ball: How the Junk Bond Machine Started the Corporate Raiders*. HarperCollins, 1989.
[4]Opler, T. and Titman, S. "The determinants of leveraged buyout activity: Free cash flow vs. financial distress costs." *Journal of Finance*, 1993.

rate for high yield bonds from 1994–2014.[5] Economic growth during the 1980s allowed early high yield issuers to prosper and for high yield by 1990 to grow into a $200 billion industry from under $10 billion just a decade earlier.[6] Increased demand opened up the possibilities for larger, more aggressive transactions. KKR's $31 billion takeover of RJR Nabisco today stands as the pinnacle of the 1980s LBO era. Financed with a staggering amount of debt, it would represent the largest buyout in history for the next 17 years. Occurring in 1989 – it would also come to symbolize the end of the 1980s LBO boom.

1.5 JUNK BONDS

In the early days of the high yield and leveraged buyout industry, meaningful data on appropriate credit metrics for buyouts did not exist. This is because the nature of the high yield issuer had changed, and performance data for this new category of issuers was limited. LBOs can put equity and debt investors at odds with each other. This is because equity investors have returns that improve with more debt, which is considered lower cost capital. This works unless of course the business becomes imperiled with such a high debt burden and defaults. Debt investors like to see larger equity investments, which to them reflect greater skin in the game and alignment. But when equity investments are low, the risk may still be attractive at a price. Ultimately, the amount of debt versus equity is a negotiation between lenders and shareholders – the two capital providers. As it turned out, early investors in high yield debt demanded high compensation for known and unknown risks but they were willing to make more risky investments than what is more typical today.

Economic growth in the 1980s, which allowed high yield issuers to perform, masked some of the risks of these transactions. But the economic recession that occurred from July 1990 to March 1991 surfaced the weak underwriting standards of many LBOs of that time. Declining credit quality had already begun to manifest itself earlier on and in 1989 default rates

---

[5]Altman Edward I. "Setting the record straight on junk bonds: A review of the research on default rates and returns." *Journal of Applied Corporate Finance*, 1990.

[6]Altman Edward I. "The high yield bond market: A decade of assessment, comparing 1990 with 2000." *NYU Stern School of Business*, 2000.

exceeded 7%. When GDP slowed and then declined, many high yield issuers simply had too much debt outstanding to withstand the economic setback. Interest expense is a significant cost to heavily indebted high yield issuers. Unlike labor, it's a fixed cost that cannot be scaled down to match economic conditions and therefore can cause companies to default and seek bankruptcy court protection. In 1990 and 1991, default rates exceeded 10%.[7] To provide some context on the damage looking back today, the cumulative default experience from 1989–1991 was worse than what was experienced during the Great Recession of 2007–2009, the most severe recession since the Great Depression and one that lasted more than twice as long as the 1990–1991 recession.

During this turbulent period in 1989 and 1990, the high yield industry suffered a number of setbacks. Some of the industry's leading advocates attracted further controversy but others crossed the line, including Michael Milken who was ultimately found guilty of violating U.S. securities laws. Drexel, the primary force behind the high yield industry, was forced into bankruptcy in 1990. Also, many high profile high yield issuers underwent restructuring that entailed employee lay-offs drawing media attention. Prominent high yield related bankruptcies during the early 1990s included Federated Department Stores, Revco Discount Drug Stores, Walter Industries, and Eaton Leonard. Although referring to high yield as "junk" was a practice that had been around for some time – it was only after this experience that the term *junk bonds* became associated with high yield debt.

For those witnessing the damage seemingly inflicted by high yield issuers, the industry appeared unruly and capable of causing great financial harm to the economy. Regulators reacted harshly with a set of rules aimed at restricting the high yield industry and improving transparency. For example, the Financial Institutions Reform, Recovery and Enforcement Act (FIRREA) of 1989 placed limitations on high yield debt investments by thrifts, or savings and loans institutions, and forced them to mark-to-market assets, which created selling pressure. The Revenue Reconciliation Act of 1989 limited the tax deductibility of certain high yield debt that lacked a cash interest component. Bank regulators issued stricter capital reserve requirements for insurance companies and other regulated financial institutions that limited their ability to participate in the market. The Securities

---

[7]Moody's Investor Service; J.P. Morgan (Default Monitor).

and Exchange Commission (SEC) encouraged the National Association of Securities Dealers (NASD) to develop and implement the Fixed Income Pricing System (FIPS), a system of tracking and reporting trading activity of high yield bonds to reduce opacity. Although most regulatory developments were aimed at curbing the use of high yield finance, improved oversight also helped restore confidence in high yield and led to more balanced growth.

1.6 MARKET MATURATION AND GROWTH

The high yield industry ultimately overcame the various scandals and regulatory setbacks because high yield debt had become an important source of capital to issuers and provided attractive risk-adjusted returns to investors. Despite high default rates and a wave of corporate bankruptcies from 1989–1991, the returns produced by the high yield asset class over this time period are not as bad as many believe. Data from Credit Suisse and Bank of America Merrill Lynch estimate the high yield market posted a positive total return in 1989 and was down 4.5%–6.5% in 1990 before recovering approximately 40% in 1991.[8] Taken alone, this data would suggest the asset class actually performed well – not just in comparison to stocks and other asset classes such as real estate – but also in relation to how high yield has performed in future recessionary periods such as the recessions of 2001 and 2007–2009. Part of the reason that high yield held up so well in 1990 is that bonds entered the year with a 15.9% yield – a 7.9% premium over comparable maturity government debt yields.[9] This hefty risk premium implied that the cost of underperformance and possible failure had largely been priced in going into the recession.

Following the junk bond market collapse, market participants organized to build a market that would function more soundly. Standard legal protections were adopted in credit agreements, business and risk disclosures improved, and new high yield issues were more carefully structured. Secondary market liquidity also improved with the adoption by the SEC of Rule 144A that facilitated trading among large institutional buyers. Credit officers, armed with the 1989–1991 downside scenario, now had an

---

[8]Bank of America Merrill Lynch Global Research; Credit Suisse.
[9]Credit Suisse.

important data point with which they could stress test capital structures to make more informed investment decisions. Lastly, private equity firms contributed more capital to LBOs to create more sound capital structures and greater alignment with creditors.

One of the key lessons learned from the 1980s LBO is the importance of a *margin of safety*. In debt investing, the margin of safety represents the amount of downside that can be sustained before the debt claim becomes impaired. One way to measure margin of safety is by way of equity contribution. To explain this through an example, if an enterprise is acquired at a fair market value, the equity contribution reflects the amount the enterprise can decline in value before the debt claim becomes impaired. In this regard, a 30% equity contribution provides a greater margin of safety than a 10% contribution. Another way to measure margin of safety is by way of debt service metrics. When debt burdens and borrowing costs are high, there is less room for a business to experience setbacks or a decline in earnings and continue to make these payments. Companies generally default on debt and seek bankruptcy protection when they can no longer service interest payments. Once a company seeks bankruptcy protection, the risk of impairment greatly increases.

When comparing the late 1980s high yield market to that of today, two noticeable differences stand out. First, debt burdens as a percentage of total enterprise value are lower now than in the past. Prior to 1990, equity contributions generally represented less than 10% of the total LBO consideration. Similar to subprime real estate loans – low equity down payments not only create an insufficient margin of safety for creditors, they also create misalignment with owners and stoke asset price bubbles. Today the amount of equity required in an LBO averages at least 25–30% of the purchase price consideration. Second, borrowing costs are also lower, primarily driven by low interest rates. The 10-year U.S. government bond in 1989 yielded almost 9% – in comparison to roughly 2% at year-end 2014. Interest rates on high yield debt are set at a premium to government rates. These two considerations imply that high yield issuers in the 1980s not only borrowed more heavily than they do today, but did so at more expensive rates.

The progression in LBO equity contribution as a percentage of the total buyout consideration is indicative of how much the high yield asset class changed following the harrowing default experiences of the early 1990s. The industry as a whole, it seems, turned its mistakes and high profile failures into a valuable learning experience. Figure 1.1 shows equity contribution as a percentage of total buyout consideration since 1987. Over

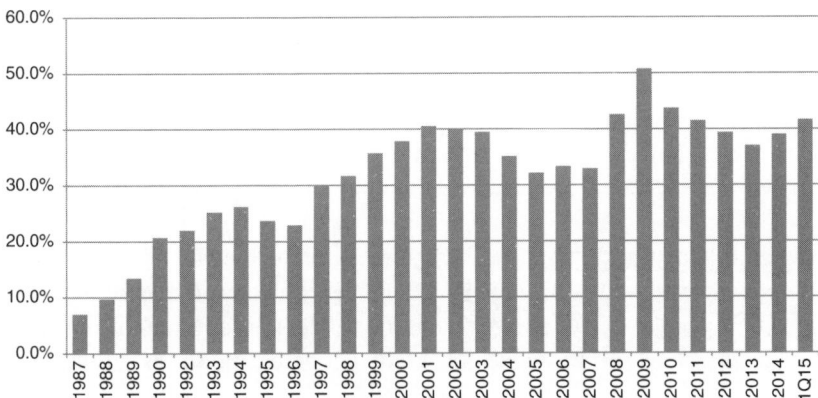

FIGURE 1.1 Trends in LBO Equity Contribution Since 1987
Note: There were too few deals in 1991 to form a meaningful sample
Source: S&P Capital IQ LCD

this 27-year time period, equity contributions in buyouts increased from under 10% to almost 40%.

While increased equity contributions has been one factor improving asset class performance, economic growth and the decline in long-term interest over the past two decades have also helped high yield issuers perform.

1.7 HIGH YIELD TODAY

High yield today is on a safer course than it was 25 years ago but the industry is still prone to both excesses and corrections, often driven by broader macroeconomic trends. Figure 1.1, on LBO equity contribution over time, highlights how equity contributions decline in the periods preceding a recession, reflecting increased risk tolerance, and then increase following a recession as lending standards become more conservative. This trend played out in the 1990–1991 recession, the 2001 recession, and then the Great Recession that lasted from December 2007 through June 2009. This of course is not just the case for high yield but for all asset classes. But what is notable about high yield is the market progression since the mid-1980s. Compared to the industry's experience in 1990–1991, future recessions did not result in the same relative magnitude of debt impairment. The overall trend in equity contribution has been especially positive – over time LBOs

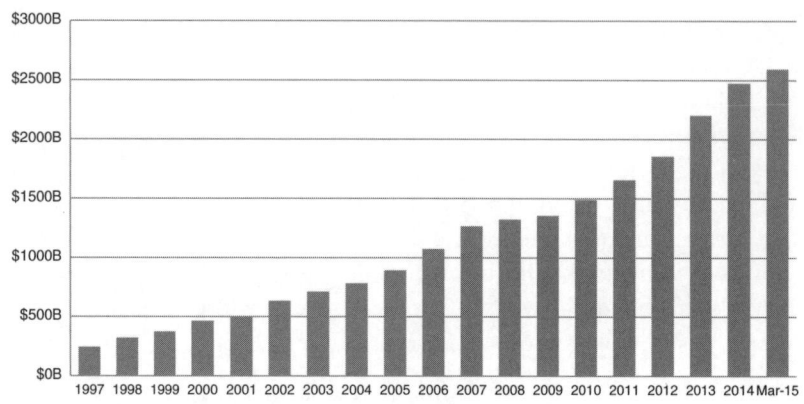

FIGURE 1.2   High Yield Debt Outstanding
Source: S&P Capital IQ LCD

have provided a greater margin of safety to debt investors. This highlights not only the more solid underpinnings of the high yield industry today but also growth and maturation in the private equity industry.

Questions will always arise regarding whether high yield valuations are appropriate or not. What is less scrutinized today is high yield's legitimacy as a source of financing for a growing number of entities including countries, municipalities, and corporations. In the United States, the corporate high yield debt market is a $2.5 trillion global industry – up 10-fold from 1997 when the market size was $243 billion.[10] High yield debt represents approximately 6% of the U.S. fixed income market. Pension funds, endowments, insurance companies, corporations, and family offices increasingly incorporate high yield debt as part of a balanced portfolio. Even individuals today can access the high yield market with daily liquidity through various retail fund offerings. Figure 1.2 highlights the extraordinary growth of the U.S corporate high yield industry since 1997.

1.8   SUMMARY

While the designation of speculative grade debt did not occur until the formation of credit rating agencies, the existence of debt of reputable businesses that hit hard times and fell out of favor is as old as

---

[10]"S&P Capital IQ LCD" – only if it is required since it is referencing the data in Figure 1.2.

capitalism. During the 1970s, a market for high yield bonds developed, which stemmed from interest in the debt of "fallen angels." Oil shocks, rising inflation, regulation, and the growth of thrifts created the backdrop for a market receptive to speculative grade primary offerings. The early issuers of high yield were in capital-intensive industries or the targets of leveraged buyouts. It took the 1990–1991 recession to expose the weak underwriting standards prevalent in the 1980s LBOs. The high yield market revived with more solid underpinnings to regain trust with a public wary of "junk bonds." Twenty years later, what was once considered a cottage industry, now represents a $2.5 trillion marketplace.

CHAPTER 2

High Yield Issuers

High yield issuers come from a broad range of industries and include household names such as Sprint, Dish Network, HCA Healthcare, Michaels Stores, J. Crew, and Dole Food Company. These companies use high yield as an alternative to other types of capital to fund growth and other transactions such as mergers and acquisitions. The two broad categories of high yield debt issued include high yield bonds and leveraged loans. When considering which type of high yield debt to raise, issuers consider their business objectives, financial prospects, and the potential risks they face. Investment banks play an important role in the high yield industry by providing issuers with advice and capital markets expertise. In this chapter we discuss the nature of high yield issuers, the decisions they make, and the capital raising process.

2.1 HIGH YIELD ISSUERS

High yield issuers come from all established sectors of the economy. They include hospital chains, casino operators, building products companies, telecommunications operators, retail chains, automotive suppliers, and media companies. What binds this group together is not only a credit rating, but also a decision to raise high yield debt. A successful retailer for example might decide to focus on a few locations, generate cash flow, and improve its credit profile. Or its growth prospects might be so compelling that it decides to carry a higher debt burden – taking its ratings below investment grade – to finance growth in new stores. Similarly, a cable operator might raise high yield bonds to expand its network and reach new underserved communities in order to fuel future growth. In these situations, the decision to raise high yield was deliberate; the issuer was willing to incur additional debt to pursue a value-enhancing opportunity.

High yield issuers can broadly be categorized by size. The smallest issuers, companies with less than $100 million of revenue and $25 million of EBITDA (earnings before interest, taxes, depreciation, and amortization), a proxy for cash flow, often must raise high yield debt through private placements. In these transactions, the owners either work directly with a few lenders or through an investment bank to raise debt that is held by one group of investors or a few investor groups. As this debt is not widely held or known of by a wider pool of investors, it is not expected to be traded in the secondary market. Buyers must be prepared to hold smaller debt offerings until they mature. This debt must therefore come at a premium to account for *illiquidity risk* or the inability to sell holdings in the secondary market without a substantial loss in value. Larger issuers, or companies who seek several hundred million or more in capital, can raise debt more efficiently through the capital markets. Investment banks solicit interest and sell this debt in smaller increments to dozens of investors, who can trade the debt with each other or investors who are new to the offering after it has been placed. Because the debt of larger offerings is liquid, or can more easily be sold in the secondary market, it results in the debt being priced on more attractive terms. Liquidity is an important consideration for certain investment funds like mutual funds and exchange traded funds (ETFs) that must be able to satisfy redemptions on a daily basis. As we discuss in later chapters, liquidity and the types of investment funds that invest in an offering also affect pricing volatility.

In this book, I focus more on the high yield market for large, distributed issues. This market is not only better tracked by industry research groups but is also what most high yield investments funds provide exposure to. The benchmark indices that provide data on asset classes on both high yield bonds set certain minimum size criteria for inclusion. For example, to be included in the Bank of America Merrill Lynch high yield index, one of the most widely followed high yield bond indices, an issue must have at least one year to maturity and $150 million or more of par value outstanding.[1] The S&P LSTA Leveraged Loan index, a commonly followed index used for tracking the leveraged loan market, tracks issuers with senior secured

---

[1]Bank of America Merrill Lynch Global Research.

U.S. denominated bank loan with a minimum initial spread of L+125 and a minimum size of $50 million.[2] It's important to keep in mind that when trends in price, spreads, and total returns are reported it's generally for the market that meets this criteria, which represents the vast majority of the high yield market.

Based on the Bank of America Merrill Lynch high yield index and S&P/LSTA Leveraged Loan index, at year-end 2014 there were over 3,500 high yield bond and leveraged loan issues outstanding in the U.S. dollar high yield market. As this high quantity suggests, high yield is a viable financing option for a large number of companies. Even foreign, multi-national corporations increasingly access the U.S. high yield market for cost-effective capital that can serve as a currency hedge for their U.S. dollar exposure. With the growth in investors participating in the high yield market, not only is the amount of high yield debt that corporations can raise greater, the liquidity or trading activity of the market has improved as well. A robust secondary market for high yield debt ultimately creates more cost-efficient capital for issuers by reducing illiquidity premiums.

Table 2.1 shows the top 10 largest high yield bond and leveraged loan offerings outstanding at year-end 2014. Many of the companies on this list are household names that most would recognize. The largest leveraged loan at $15.5 billion was issued by TXU Energy, a Texas-based utility company. TXU was acquired by KKR, Texas Pacific Group, and Goldman Sachs Capital Partners in 2007 for $45 billion and represents the largest buyout in history. The largest bond outstanding at S4.2 billion was issued by Sprint Corporation, which is a publicly owned company with stock that trades on the New York Stock Exchange.

Large high yield issues are quite attractive to many high yield investors. Due to their size and liquidity profile, they become common holdings for large funds invested in the market such as mutual funds. This occurs for a few reasons. The first and most obvious one is that the largest funds have to invest significant amounts of capital and large issues provide a means to do so. Second, many funds that provide high yield exposure, such as mutual funds and ETFs, provide their investors with *daily liquidity* or the ability to redeem capital with one day's notice. This liquidity is actually required for funds to meet legal regulation related to many types of publicly offered funds. To meet such redemptions, which can be unexpected, the fund's

---

[2]S&P Capital IQ LCD.

TABLE 2.1 Largest High Yield Bond and Leveraged Loan Issues

Top 10 Largest High Yield Bond Issues		Top 10 Largest Leveraged Loan Issues	
High Yield Bonds	**Issue Size ($M)**	**Leveraged Loans**	**Issue Size ($M)**
Sprint	$4,250	TXU Energy	$15,528
Caesars Entertainment	$3,681	Burger King Corp.	$6,750
Reynolds Group Issuer	$3,250	H.J. Heinz Company	$6,468
H.J. Heinz Company	$3,100	Energy Future Intermediate	$5,400
Chrysler Group LLC	$3,080	Hilton Hotels	$5,100
Community Health Systems	$3,000	Clear Channel Communications	$5,000
HCA Healthcare	$3,000	Fortescue Metals Group	$4,901
First Data Corporation	$3,000	Dell Inc.	$4,613
Chrysler Group LLC	$2,875	First Data Corporation	$4,600
Tenet Healthcare	$2,800	Avago Technologies	$4,577

Note: As of December 31, 2014
Source: J.P. Morgan (High Yield Bonds), S&P Capital IQ LCD (Leveraged Loans)

manager must choose between selling holdings, borrowing, or using cash. Mutual funds therefore are often willing to accept lower returns for larger high yield issues that maintain good liquidity – they provide an easier means to match the sometimes fast-changing needs of their investor base. Last, large issues are more important constituents in high yield indices. By maintaining investments in these issues, high yield funds can minimize *tracking error,* a measure of how closely a portfolio follows the index to which it is benchmarked. A good number of high yield funds are focused on replicating the index return or, ideally, doing a little better. These types of funds are more humorously referred to as *index* or *benchmark huggers.* Collectively, these attributes make large issues appealing to a large number of investment funds that participate in the high yield market.

But not all investors are interested in the largest and most liquid issues. In fact, the very attributes that make them attractive to large funds is what makes them unattractive to other investor groups. For example, credit hedge funds generally do not provide their investors with the ability to redeem capital daily. As a result, they can afford to take more illiquidity risk. It is often the smaller issues with less liquidity that offer greater return compensation. High yield issues may vary considerably in size but large and smaller issues alike still find a home as the investor base is broad and varied, operating with different investment mandates and return expectations.

2.2 CAPITAL STRUCTURE CONSIDERATIONS

Understanding the concept of capital structure helps explain why companies choose to raise high yield bonds and leveraged loans in varying combinations. A *capital structure* is the mix of debt and equity that a company has outstanding. It shows the type of capital that has been used to finance a company's operations. A related concept to capital structure is *enterprise value*. An enterprise value is the sum of all debt and equity in the capital structure, less balance sheet cash. For example, if a company has $700 million of debt and $300 million of equity, its enterprise value is $1 billion less any balance sheet cash. As equity claims are junior in right of payment to debt claims, many debt investors consider the equity portion of an enterprise value the margin of safety or the amount the company's value could decline before the debt becomes impaired or worth less than 100%. Using our previous example, the enterprise could be worth $300 million less – the amount of equity – before the debt would incur principal losses.

A company's capital structure provides insights on how shareholders believe they can best maximize future business value. This is because capital structures are by nature subjective decisions; a company can usually raise debt and equity in multiple combinations and usually there is no one right solution. However, there are some general guidelines that are followed. In a leveraged buyout (LBO), for example, a capital structure will often consist of 70% debt and 30% equity. LBOs usually target more established businesses that can support a relatively high debt burden. The debt provides a means to gain ownership with a lower upfront investment. In contrast, early stage, venture capital backed companies have greater uncertainty and risk of failure and therefore are usually capitalized entirely with equity to provide maximum business flexibility.

There have been many studies conducted on optimal capital structure construction. In my own experience, I find that in the high yield market – where companies are more indebted – capital structures reflect a company's need to balance these two somewhat opposing goals. The first goal relates to minimizing the cost of capital to the issuer. Obviously, no firm wants to pay more for capital than it has to. The second relates to maximizing business flexibility, to provide room for growth and business setbacks. The challenge with the two goals is that they can run counter to each other. A low-cost capital structure consists mostly of debt, which can imperil a business in downside scenarios, and a capital structure that maximizes business flexibility consists mostly of equity. Equity has a higher cost of capital than debt based on its expected return. Without the use of lower cost debt, it is difficult for equity investors, who are the company's shareholders, to obtain sufficient returns when buying or growing more established businesses.

The three components of a high yield issuer's capital structure are leveraged loans, high yield bonds, and equity. The difference between these three sources of capital relates primarily to payment priority, which reflects risk and cost. Leveraged loans are usually the first to be repaid, and therefore have the lowest risk and cost. Bonds are next in line, followed by equity. Equity capital, such as that provided by private equity firms, has the highest risk-reward potential because it is junior in right of payment to all debt but retains all residual enterprise value after the repayment of debt claims. If a business's enterprise value grows by 50% – for example, a $1 billion enterprise grows to $1.5 billion, the debt will receive its contractual principal and interest payments while the equity stands to profit more significantly from all residual upside. Conversely, if the enterprise value declines by 20%, the equity faces losses while the debt may still receive its principal and interest. The varying risk-reward of these three capital structure components – loans, bond, and equity – attracts different investor types. By appealing to investors with different risk tolerance, or essentially parsing and distributing risk to more natural buyers, issuers can construct more cost-efficient capital structures.

2.3 CHOOSING BETWEEN HIGH YIELD BONDS AND LEVERAGED LOANS

High yield bonds and leveraged loans are the two broad categories of below investment grade debt. There are various types of loans and bonds, which we discuss in later chapters. But the basic differences between the two are that bonds are most often fixed-rate obligations, paying interest at a set rate for the term of the debt, and are generally long-term obligations with less flexibility for early repayment. Leveraged loans are commonly floating-rate liabilities, paying interest at a spread to *LIBOR*. The interest rate on loans resets periodically, often monthly or quarterly and thereby provides protection to investors from rising interest rates. In comparison to bonds, loans generally have shorter term maturities and fewer or no penalties for early repayment. Loans also come with more restrictive terms than bonds to lessen risk. Due to these attributes, issuers usually pay less to issue loans versus bonds.

High yield issuers work with investment bankers to determine whether to raise leveraged loans, high yield bonds, or some combination of the two. One of the primary considerations in this decision relates to the nature of the business. For example, if a business is recessionary-resistant, well-diversified and fast-growing, a low-cost capital structure that maximizes leveraged loan borrowings may be valued most. This business could use its cash flow to repay debt borrowings and lower its interest burden and expense over time. In contrast, a highly cyclical business that seeks to invest its cash flow into growth opportunities may want longer-term capital with more flexibility, which they could achieve with bonds. Another important consideration relates to capital market conditions. In buoyant and low interest-rate market environments, creditors are often willing to lend on more attractive terms, which can affect the amount of debt available as well as its interest rate or cost. This may make it appealing to raise long-term bonds and lock-in low borrowing costs for the long term. In less favorable market conditions, investors may be more risk averse and the opposite holds true.

To explain this by way of an example, if a $1 billion enterprise was highly stable and cash flow generative, cost of capital would be emphasized over business flexibility. The optimal capital structure might consist of a $400 million term loan, $300 million high yield bond, and $300 million of common equity. This would provide some pre-payable debt in the form of loans as well as some long-term capital in the form of bonds. On the other hand, if the business was cyclical, more capital intensive, and needed greater flexibility to prosper in tougher times, the optimal capital structure might include $700 million of bonds and $300 million of equity. Using bonds instead of loans allows the issuer to benefit from longer term debt maturities, a set interest rate, and no debt repayment requirements prior to maturity. However, the bonds would be very costly to prepay early, as they

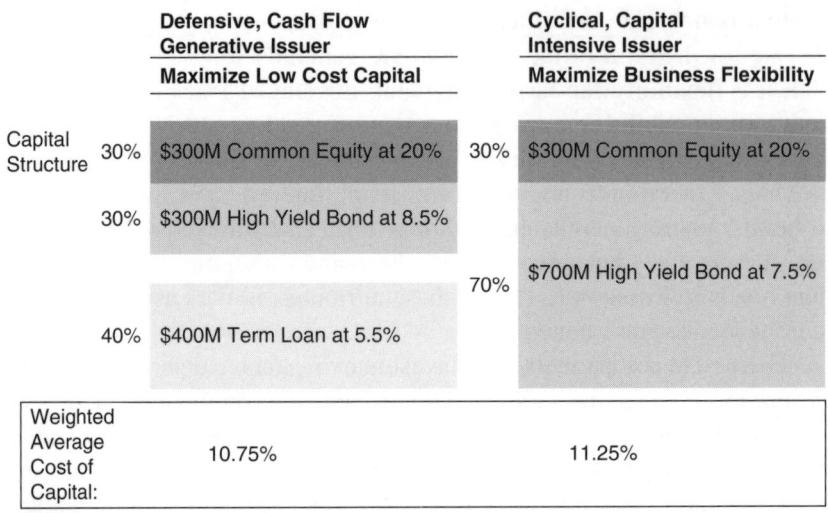

FIGURE 2.1   High Yield Capital Structures

have what's called a no-call provision, which essentially imposes a hefty monetary penalty to the issuer if it seeks to repay early. This is done to ensure the bond has a minimum duration. Key economic features of high yield debt are discussed in later chapters. For now it's just important to know that loans allow more flexibility for early repayment than bonds and therefore are favored by cash flow generative businesses. Figure 2.1 shows how these two capital structures compare.

Ultimately, it's up to owners to decide on the optimal mix of debt and equity in the capital structure of the company. The goal is to enable growth and reduce capital costs without overly impeding downside flexibility. As the industry has learned from experience, high debt capitalizations are not healthy for businesses or investors. Companies invariably experience setbacks – like losing a major customer, new competition, new or more stringent regulation, or lower business demand resulting from an economic recession. When this occurs, businesses with excessive debt must take aggressive actions to reduce costs, oftentimes actions that cut into the bones of a company and prevent a full recovery. Businesses with less or no leverage have more flexibility to weather difficult times. Debt can improve equity returns and create businesses with scale advantages, but that must be balanced against the risk of more limited business flexibility during periods of stress.

2.4 HIGH YIELD ISSUERS BY INDUSTRY

There is much overlap between the industries that issue high yield bonds and leverage loans. For example, at year-end 2014, companies in the media and telecom industries were the most prolific users of high yield debt. Many of these companies have business models that require significant capital to stay competitive by upgrading networks and content. Creditors lend to these companies because they have recurring and predictable cash flow streams built on subscriptions and tangible and intellectual property that can be pledged as collateral and sold in downside scenarios.

Table 2.2 compares industry exposures of the high yield bond versus leveraged loan indices. Differences in industry exposure illustrate how leveraged loans and high yield bonds can appeal to different types of issuers. It is also one of many reasons why these two market segments – high yield bonds and leveraged loans – can perform differently over the same time period. Cyclical industries – like energy, financials, metals/mining, transportation, and housing – are more heavily represented with bonds than loans. One of the most notable differences in industry exposure in 2014 was the oil and gas sector which represented 15% of the high yield bond market versus 4% of the leveraged loan market. In the second half of 2014, oil prices dropped from over $100 to approximately $50 per barrel. During this time period, the high yield bond market was more negatively affected by the oil price decline than the leveraged loan market. This is one example of why, despite what many still believe, not all high yield exposure is the same.

2.5 PURPOSE OF HIGH YIELD DEBT

High yield is most commonly originated to support four transaction types: mergers and acquisitions, project financings, leveraged recapitalizations, and refinancings. *Mergers and acquisitions (M&A)* involve buying, selling, or combining different companies. Often in the form of an LBO, the goal of M&A is to improve the acquired business, grow earnings, and later sell the ownership stake at a higher valuation.

The LBO industry is a major driver of high yield new issuance and is supported by the private equity industry, which provides the equity to support or "sponsor" buyouts. Private equity firms for this reason are also

TABLE 2.2 Outstanding High Yield Debt by Industry

High Yield Bond Index		Leveraged Loan Index	
Industry	% Total Market Value	Industry	% Total Market Value
Energy	16.6%	Healthcare	11.9%
Healthcare	8.8%	Technology	10.7%
Financial	7.3%	Services	9.3%
Technology	6.6%	Gaming Lodging and Leisure	7.5%
Services	5.1%	Retail	6.2%
Gaming Lodging and Leisure	5.1%	Industrials	5.9%
Metals and Mining	4.9%	Food and Beverages	5.3%
Housing	4.8%	Diversified Media	4.2%
Retail	4.6%	Chemicals	4.2%
Industrials	4.5%	Utility	4.1%
Cable and Satellite	3.9%	Cable and Satellite	3.9%
Telecommunications	3.9%	Energy	3.6%
Food and Beverages	3.6%	Financial	3.4%
Paper and Packaging	3.2%	Broadcasting	3.2%
Automotive	3.2%	Telecommunications	3.1%
Utility	2.9%	Automotive	2.8%
Chemicals	2.9%	Consumer Products	2.6%
Diversified Media	2.4%	Transportation	2.3%
Broadcasting	2.3%	Paper and Packaging	2.2%
Consumer Products	2.1%	Metals and Mining	2.1%
Transportation	1.2%	Housing	1.4%

Note: As of December 31, 2014
Source: J.P. Morgan

called *financial sponsors*. As of June 30, 2014, there was roughly $535 billion of "dry powder," or cash raised by private equity firms available to invest in leveraged buyouts.[3] This capital, which is committed and available for investment over many years, suggests that LBOs will continue to be a driver of high yield issuance for the foreseeable future.

---

[3] *Pitchbook Report*, 2014.

A *leveraged recapitalization* or *leveraged recap* is simply a transaction where high yield is raised to fund a distribution to owners. This occurs more often with established high yield issuers that have performed well and have reduced leverage as a result. A proven business that has met defined objectives will generate goodwill with its lenders who might then provide more capital, even if that capital creates no economic value to the company. *Project financings* include capital intensive business expansions such as a large casino operator raising high yield to finance the construction of a new casino site. Of all the reasons high yield issuers raise debt, however, refinancing existing high yield debt is the most common.

Refinancing of existing debt can represent over 50% of high yield new issue volume, particularly in the years following a recession when borrowings rates are low and maturities need to be extended.[4] The high volume accounted for by refinancing reflects the fact that most high yield issuers do not expect to repay debt from operating cash flow. Instead, they expect the business to be sold, taken public through an initial public offering (IPO), or for liabilities to be refinanced at lower rates as the business performs. High yield issuers are more often dynamic enterprises with owners usually seeking some type of transformative event in a five-year time period. As a result, debt maturities, which often range from 5 to 10 years, become more of an issue for underperforming companies or during economic downturns, which not only can cause businesses to decline in value but may also limit refinancing and M&A activity.

When considering growth of the high yield market, it's important to keep in mind that refinancing activity does not net much new supply. Refinancings are often supported by existing lenders who *rollover* their exposure, which is another way of saying that they maintain a similar holding in the new deal. Growth in the high yield market is primarily driven by non-refinancing new issue volume.

Figure 2.2 compares historical new issue loan volume against default rates to highlight the cyclical nature of new issuance. As depicted, new issue volume soars during periods of economic growth, ultimately leading to more aggressive transactions as confidence builds. When recessions occur, such as the December 2007 through June 2009 Great Recession, new issue volume drops, often precipitously. This highlights how difficult

---

[4]S&P Capital IQ LCD.

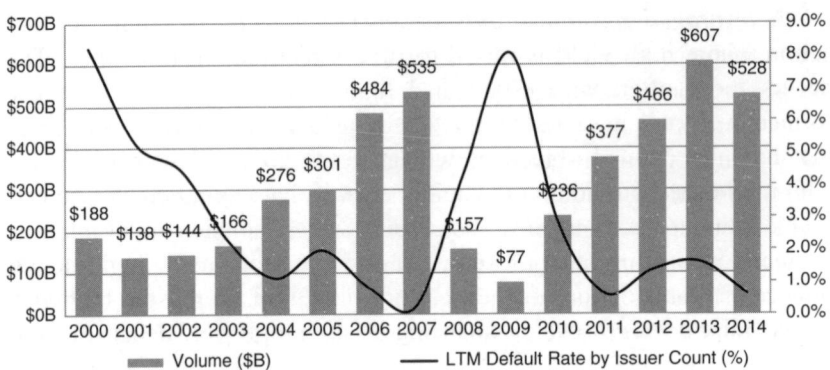

FIGURE 2.2   New Issue Loan Volume vs. Annual Default Rates
Source: S&P Capital IQ LCD

the high yield market can be to access during downturns and periods of risk aversion. Less open capital markets can exacerbate defaults, as they did in 2008, particularly as issuers struggle to refinance near-term liabilities. When the economy begins to recover as it did in 2010, refinancing related volume usually represents the largest transaction type by volume, in part because it does not require new demand but also in part because interest rates are low following a recession and this creates opportunity to refinance more expensive debt with lower cost borrowings and extend maturities.

2.6   THE ROLE OF INVESTMENT BANKS

Investment banks are important financial intermediaries for high yield issuers and facilitate a wide variety of financial transactions including IPOs, mergers and acquisitions, and capital raises. The largest investment banks include J.P. Morgan, Barclays, Bank of America Merrill Lynch, Goldman Sachs, Deutsche Bank, Morgan Stanley, UBS, Credit Suisse, and Citibank. All of these banks are actively involved in the high yield market. In addition, there are a number of smaller investment banks and more boutique firms such as Imperial Capital, Jefferies, and Guggenheim Securities that also participate to a varying extent in high yield origination and market-making.

Investment banks operate with a broker-dealer license which allows them to provide investment advice, raise capital, and make secondary markets for trading following the primary issuance. Most high yield issuers are in frequent discussions with high yield investment bankers for updates on market conditions and opportunities to enhance their capital structure. When issuers require new capital, investments banks will often *underwrite* an offering, or provide committed financing. This is a valuable service, as most transactions require committed financing to advance.

For buyers of high yield, investment banks also provide a number of services, which ultimately benefit issuers. Following a primary issuance, investment banks will make a market in the high yield issue. Unlike the stock market, there is less regulation governing market-making of high yield debt. For example, if a bank no longer wants to make a market in a high yield bond, it does not have to. This flexibility, as a result of a lighter regulatory touch can, however, cause high yield to become illiquid, particularly during periods of risk aversion. However, investment banks who underwrite and sell offerings, work to facilitate secondary market liquidity in the issues they are involved with. This is because it's good practice to support an underwritten deal and also because it's profitable. When an investment bank syndicates a leveraged loan or a bond to a group of investors, it develops a good relationship with the buyer base. This positions the underwriter well to garner secondary trading volume, which provides profitable and often risk-free trading revenue.

Another service some investment banks provide to high yield buyers is *prime brokerage*. Prime brokerage involves providing financing for debt purchases and *securities borrowing* for short selling, among other things. The amount and cost of financing available from investment banks can have an impact on market conditions for new issues by increasing or decreasing demand. In this regard, regulation that impacts the cost of banks providing financing for high yield debt can have important implications on demand for new issues and therefore issuer borrowing costs.

Ultimately, by supporting both buyers and issuers of high yield, investment banks wield significant influence over the market. When investment banks are financially healthy and optimistic on the market outlook, secondary liquidity, financing and the terms of new issuance can all improve. When investments banks are under pressure to raise capital, like they were in 2008 during the financial crisis, it can limit issuers' access to the capital markets and create a market environment characterized by forced selling and illiquidity, particularly as investor credit lines get pulled. The health of investment banks and the regulatory capital environment are important factors impacting the proper functioning of the high yield market.

2.7 THE HIGH YIELD CAPITAL RAISING PROCESS

The process for raising high yield capital through the capital markets is fairly standard for high yield bonds and leveraged loans and occurs with great frequency. On most days, a new high yield bond or leveraged loan offering is announced. But by the time of this announcement, which signals the launching of a marketing process by an investment bank, most of the decisions pertaining to the capital raise and its terms have already been decided.

Investment banks work with the sponsors and issuers of high yield transactions at early stages to help determine the type of high yield debt to raise, the amounts, and expected cost and terms. In the case of an LBO, a private equity firm that is competing to buy a business in an auction process will obtain committed financing from an investment bank prior to making its final bid. Final bids in competitive processes usually allow for few outs, and therefore capital commitments provided by investment banks must account for as many details as possible.

Investment banks' financing commitments come in various forms. In an *underwritten offering* or *committed financing*, an investment bank or group of investment banks commit to raise the financing or act as a lender of last resort. This type of commitment provides the most certainty and is most often sought by issuers. A *best efforts* underwriting is one where the investment bank does its best to sell the issue but has no obligation to buy it should demand prove insufficient. Best efforts commitments more often occur in volatile markets or with opportunistic transactions that have a more questionable probability of success. For larger transactions, it is common to see investments banks work in concert with each other to reduce the amount of capital any one party has to put at risk. More banks being involved with an offering can also facilitate better secondary market liquidity, which is an investor consideration as it can reduce illiquidity premiums and therefore results in a lower cost of funds to the issuer.

Investment banks compete for high yield financings based on their track record, the fees they will charge, and the terms under which they are willing to underwrite the debt offering. In an ideal scenario, the new issue is well received by investors and fully distributed. However, between the time of a commitment and the time of launching a marketing process, markets and businesses can change. Or sometimes, the investment banks and sponsors wrongly forecast how investors will react to an offering. In the case where there is insufficient demand for a high yield offering, the terms under which the bank will own the debt matter most. Ultimately, with any committed financing, the sponsor must be comfortable proceeding on the underwritten terms, which are less favorable than what all parties expect to achieve but important downside modeling considerations when assessing potential profits.

When a high yield issuer selects an investment bank or a group of banks to raise high yield capital, several factors go into determining the amount of debt, interest rate, and other applicable terms. An important factor taken into account for a new issue transaction is the history of the issuer in the high yield market – the question, put another way, is are they a *seasoned* or *debut* issuer? If they are seasoned, key questions will be how well the debt performed for investors and whether the company met its budget. If they are a debut issuer, the debt of comparable businesses can provide a benchmark for the interest rate and leverage obtainable.

Investment banks perform extensive analyses and report to internal credit committees, which evaluate all key aspects of the deal before permitting the making of any commitments. In addition to the performance of the company over a business cycle, their analysis will consider comparable deals in the industry, and not only how well those deals have performed but also where that debt is trading, which provides important insights on pricing. Even deals that are not in the industry but are recent issues with comparable estimated ratings can provide insights on investor demand. Additional factors that are relevant include the track record of the private equity sponsor (if applicable), industry classification, business model risks and growth prospects, EBITDA, free cash flow generation, and proposed credit metrics of the issuer.

To market new issues, investment bankers work with the company to prepare an *offering memorandum*. The offering memorandum provides important information related to the debt offering including the transaction structure, credit highlights, business and financial profile, and legal terms. For bonds, this document is also known as a *prospectus;* for leveraged loans it's often called a *bank book*. Offering memorandums are disseminated to hundreds of prospective investors. As part of the marketing process, management meetings are arranged, sometimes in several cities, in a process called the *management roadshow*. These meetings provide investors with an opportunity to meet management in person and ask questions directly. Sometimes, where the need to generate investor support justifies it, even site visits to key operational facilities are organized.

Following the roadshow, investors complete their due diligence on the debt offering. Interested parties then provide investment commitments, which are tallied up by participating investment banks. If commitments are too low, the deal is considered *under-subscribed* and pricing and terms are *flexed* or enhanced to induce greater investor participation. If an offering is *over-subscribed*, then pricing is *reverse-flexed* or tightened to benefit the issuer. Following any flex activity, investors recommit and the investment bank allocates the offering in consultation with the issuer.

Pricing high yield transactions is an art that requires a careful understanding of the buyer base and market environment. Underwriters often seek to set pricing at a level where accounts are under-allocated. This creates follow-on demand in the secondary market that supports some price appreciation. If the debt appreciates too significantly, the owners might think they paid too much for the capital and that the underwriter mispriced the deal. That might jeopardize the investment bank's ability to win future mandates, which is a meaningful consideration particularly with large and active private equity sponsors. In my opinion, the goal of investment banks should be to strike a reasonable balance between issuers and investors. With a small amount of price appreciation, early investors are rewarded for participating in the new offering and are more likely to subscribe to the next deal.

2.8 SUMMARY

High yield issuers are well-established companies spanning a broad range of industries and include many household names. These issuers tap the high yield market for high yield bonds and/or leveraged loans to finance mergers and acquisitions, leveraged recapitalization and project financings. However, in most years, the primary reason high yield is raised is to refinance existing debt. New issue volume is highly sensitive to economic conditions and default rates. It is also sensitive to the regulatory environment and health of investment banks, which are financial intermediaries that provide capital raising services for issuers and facilitate secondary trading for investors.

CHAPTER 3

Buying High Yield Debt

Buyers of high yield debt are attracted to its relatively high interest rate and at times the possibility of capital appreciation. Increasingly, groups such as pension funds, insurance companies, family offices, and retirees have deployed assets into high yield debt funds to generate current income to fund existing obligations. As we discuss in this chapter, high yield bonds cannot be easily purchased by individual investors. It is a market that is traded over-the-counter and more the domain of large, institutional investors. That being said, there are numerous funds that provide high yield exposure to smaller investors and it is possible, to a limited extent, to source individual issues. When buying high yield debt, it's first important to appreciate how performance variations of high yield's two market segments – high yield bonds and leverage loans – can vary and be driven by the investment mandates of its buyers and the types of financing employed. Particularly after the Great Recession – a period of unprecedented volatility in the high yield market – it has become increasingly important for investors to understand the impact of collateralized loan obligations (CLOs) and margin finance on the high yield asset class.

3.1 WHO CAN BUY HIGH YIELD BONDS?

As a security governed by the Securities Act of 1933, a registered high yield bond can be bought by both individuals and institutional investors. In practice, however, it is less common for individuals to buy high yield bonds, especially in the primary or new issue market for two reasons. First, high yield bonds are distributed by Wall Street firms over-the-counter and therefore only investors who have an established trading relationship can participate in the offering. As Wall Street firms are generally looking to distribute issues in increments of a million dollars or more, they tend to work with institutional investors. Second, most high yield bonds are privately placed by those same Wall Street firms pursuant to *Rule 144A* promulgated in early 1990s under the Securities Act, to *qualified institutional buyers (QIBs)*, which are U.S. institutional investors that own at least $100 million of securities, among other qualifying factors. They include large retail fund managers, pension funds, large family offices, and insurance companies. QIBs constitute the largest buyers of high yield bonds and, under Rule 144A, have the ability to freely trade non-registered bonds with each other. This market among QIBs is considered private, as it is inaccessible to the general public, and requires investors who through their sheer size demonstrate that they are sophisticated and cognizant of the risks of trading in private securities.

If a high yield bond is distributed pursuant to Rule 144A (and no other company securities are publicly traded), the issuer is exempt from publicly filing financial statements with the Securities and Exchange Commission (SEC). It is worth noting that a high yield issuer accessing capital via Rule 144A often does so to avoid public reporting requirements. When an issuer reports financial statements with the SEC, sensitive information becomes available for competitors, customers, suppliers, and regulators to scrutinize. Further, following the implementation of the Sarbanes–Oxley Act of 2002, the cost of complying with public reporting standards increased and the penalties for non-compliance became more severe. The avoidance of reporting requirements leads to a market that can be said to lack transparency, but this opacity indirectly leads to some important cost and operating benefits to issuers. At the same time, many high yield issuers use Rule 144A issuances to access capital more quickly and then, sometimes, agree to file public statements at a later date, usually within 180 to 540 days from the initial offering. This type of offering is known as a *144A offering with registration rights*. Owners of the Rule 144A-issued bonds can later exchange their bonds for registered notes in so-called A/B exchange offers that make those bonds publicly tradable. This can be important to some buyers. Since most of the 144A-issued bonds are exchanged for registered bonds (with few limited exceptions for affiliate and market-makers), the size of the issue, as exchanged, remains practically the same, allowing the issue to maintain its liquidity.

A substantial portion of the high yield bond market is sold to QIBs via Rule 144A or another exemption under the Securities Act known as Regulation S (popularly known as Reg S), which is available to foreign buyers. Some bonds, however, are registered and can be bought similarly to public equities through a retail brokerage firm like Morgan Stanley or Charles Schwab. The brokerage firms can source small bond offerings, also known as *odd lots*, through their access to the high yield market. The selection of bonds available for retail investment is generally limited and the prices are often several points higher than what institutional investors pay. When buying "retail," an investor often pays two commissions, one to its broker and another to the broker that is selling the bonds. As a result, if a non-institutional buyer's goal is to build a diversified portfolio of high yield holdings, it is often more efficient to invest directly through larger funds that buy "wholesale."

3.2 WHO CAN BUY LEVERAGED LOANS?

Legally, leveraged loans can be bought by accredited investors, or individuals who meet certain net worth requirements that are lower than QIB requirements, but that rarely occurs. Similar to high yield bonds, leveraged loans are sold and traded over-the-counter by investment banks. Investment banks perform due diligence on all trading partners including *know-your-customer (KYC)* requirements. This process is conducted by internal compliance departments to ensure that the bank is not violating any U.S. laws. Most investment banks do not want to transact with small, potentially unsophisticated buyers who are not profitable enough for the bank to support with sales coverage. As a result, major Wall Street investment banks generally require that any leveraged loan counter-party also be a QIB. The result is that individual investors or institutions not set up to transact with Wall Street banks directly, can only gain leveraged loan exposure through a hedge fund, mutual fund, ETF, or closed-end fund that focuses on leveraged loans.

3.3 BUYERS OF HIGH YIELD DEBT

High yield bonds and leveraged loans have developed distinct buyer bases over time. Since the early days of the high yield market, bonds have

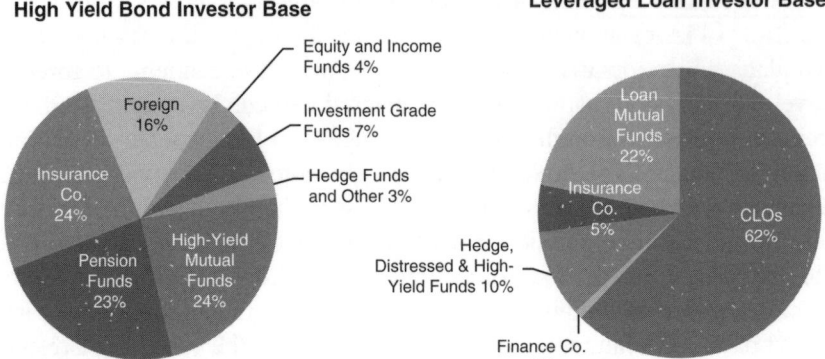

FIGURE 3.1 High Yield Bond and Leveraged Loan Buyers
Note: As of December 31, 2014
Source: J.P. Morgan (High Yield Bond Investor Base), S&P Capital IQ LCD
(Leveraged Loan Investor Base)

primarily been held by institutional buyers. Leverage loans in contrast, up until the mid-1990s, were mostly bought and held by commercial banks. This is one of the reasons why leveraged loans today pay interest on a spread to LIBOR. At the time, a floating rate of interest was required for banks to match fund assets with liabilities. But regulatory developments, starting with Basel I, also known as the 1988 Basel Accord, have helped institutionalize the leveraged loan market. Basel I required banks to set aside more capital for higher risk assets such as corporate debt. This made the business of originating and holding leveraged loans less attractive and encouraged innovation. By the late 1990s, Wall Street had begun to distribute and trade leveraged loans in a manner similar to high yield bonds.

Two developments that helped facilitate the transition from a buy-and-hold to a syndicated leveraged loan market are (1) the introduction of market flex, a provision that allows underwriters to modify economic and legal terms of the debt to reduce distribution risk and (2) the development of structured finance, or vehicles that could more easily buy loans with financing. As loans are not a security that can be financed with margin, more creative financing structures such as *collateralized loan obligations* (*CLOs*) had to be developed to open up the asset class to a broader group of investors. Figure 3.1 highlights the differences between the high yield bond and leverage loan buyer bases.

3.4 INVESTMENT MANDATES IMPACT VOLATILITY

Understanding the market participants that invest in high yield bonds and loans is critical to understanding asset class performance, especially in stressed market environments. The buyer base for high yield bonds as shown in Figure 3.1 is more dispersed and consists primarily of what I consider *relative value* investors or investors who evaluate risk-return across a broad range of asset classes and therefore source opportunities more broadly. Relative value, which compares the risk-return of one asset class to another, is an important consideration for large institutions that can invest broadly across assets including bonds, real estate, stocks, and commodities. There are certain buyers of high yield bonds such as pension funds, insurance companies, and institutions that will always maintain some exposure to high yield but that exposure amount can vary over time. Relative value investors buy when they see value and can reduce exposure more quickly as better opportunities in other markets surface. As a result of its buyers having broad investment mandates, high yield bonds can experience periods of significant volatility as capital moves in and out of the asset class.

Leveraged loans tend to be less volatile than bonds for a few reasons. First, most leveraged loans represent more senior claims in the capital structure with greater principal safety than bonds. As a result, fundamental value and the prospect of impairment are called into question less. Second, unlike high yield bonds, loans cannot be traditionally shorted and therefore are subject to less price speculation. Last, the investor base for loans consists of more committed rather than relative value investors, because the investment mandates of the buyers only permit for fund investments to be made primarily in leveraged loans. This is best evidenced by the fact that over 60% of institutional leveraged loans are bought by *CLOs*.[1] Discussed in more detail below, CLOs are structured finance vehicles that have long term capital and invest predominantly in leveraged loans (a CLO manager, for example, cannot invest in equities or other asset classes, its investment mandate makes it more committed to the leveraged loan asset class). An additional 20% of the institutional leveraged loan investor base consists of leveraged loan mutual funds that are also committed to the asset class because they have an explicit mandate to invest in leveraged loans.[2]

---

[1] S&P Capital IQ LCD.
[2] Ibid.

"Retail funds" or those available to individual investors such as ETFs, closed-end funds, and mutual funds have the potential to exacerbate market volatility. Discussed in Chapter 9, these types of funds by statute must provide investors with an ability to redeem their holdings daily. Daily liquidity is a nice feature, but for a $2.5 trillion asset class that trades $10–$30 billion a day it can sometimes force price discovery on issues at times when investors are better sellers, which can lead to quicker pricing declines. Hedge funds can also exacerbate market volatility by quickly moving in and out of markets, shorting on the downside and aggressively using leverage to fund investments (which can result in margin calls and forced selling in down markets).

Table 3.1 highlights how the composition of investors in the leveraged loan market has changed over time. In 2014, CLOs and loan mutual funds were big players while banks and hedge funds had greatly reduced their holdings of leveraged loans over the past 5 years. These types of changes are significant and can provide insight on future market volatility.

3.5 COLLATERALIZED LOAN OBLIGATIONS (CLOs)

Collateralized loan obligations (CLOs) buy a pool of leveraged loans and finance that purchase with tranches of debt and equity with varying payment priority. CLOs generally own 140–170 loans with primarily BB and B ratings.[3] The pool of assets CLOs hold is diverse, with the top 10 holdings generally representing less than 7.5% of total assets, and the top 50 holdings representing less than 25%.[4] To finance the purchase of these assets, a CLO structure raises capital with varying risk-reward. The senior-most capital, or the capital that is first to be repaid, has a AAA credit rating which implies the risk of default loss is negligible. This capital might be provided by insurance companies or banks that can borrow inexpensively and profit from the spread. The CLO structure seeks to minimize the cost of financing by maximizing lower cost, higher rated liabilities. The next tier of capital raised are rated AA. As more junior capital is raised, the risk profile increases, which must be compensated by higher return. In this way, the CLO structure parses the risk-reward associated with the pool of leveraged loan assets and its income stream to different buyers.

---

[3]Wells Fargo Research.
[4]Ibid.

TABLE 3.1 Shifts in the Leveraged Loan Buyer Base

Primary Market Investor Base	2004	2005	2006	2007	2008	2009	2010	2011	2012	2013	2014
Hedge/Distressed	6%	8%	13%	22%	23%	21%	26%	24%	20%	8%	9%
Loan Mutual Funds	12%	12%	10%	7%	4%	6%	12%	15%	13%	27%	19%
CLOs	42%	45%	48%	48%	37%	34%	35%	33%	48%	45%	55%
Banks & Sec. Firms	30%	26%	20%	17%	28%	30%	18%	19%	13%	14%	10%
Other	10%	9%	8%	5%	8%	8%	9%	9%	6%	7%	6%

Source: S&P Capital IQ LCD

The junior-most claims in the CLO structure are considered "equity." Unlike the other claims, the equity has no interest rate but rather profits from what is known as the *CLO arbitrage*, or the difference between the yield on the assets less the yield on the liabilities, which can be significant given the amount of debt that can be raised in CLO structures. Most CLOs today have significant portfolio overlap, a result of the diversification and ratings requirements of these vehicles. And much of the portfolio's assets are simply covering the costs of the liabilities. However, the 10%–20% of a CLO's portfolio that differs across managers, and can have higher risk-reward attributes, is often what drives the excess spread or CLO arbitrage. It can also be a source of performance deviations across managers. Table 3.2 shows a sample CLO structure at the time of writing. The table shows the mix of debt and equity funding by amount, rating, and spread.

It is important to realize that a CLO capitalization sources from a wide investor base seeking attractive return relative to ratings. AAA buyers can get higher yields with CLO liabilities than available from other AAA instruments – this is called a *ratings arbitrage*. The arbitrage results from several factors with a primary consideration being the smaller, more illiquid size of the CLO liability tranche. When ascribing ratings to the various debt tranches, rating agencies consider what amount of defaults can occur before principal or interest is impaired. Because defaulted loans have experienced a long-term recovery rate of approximately 70%, CLO capitalizations generally have AAA liabilities at a level under 70%. This essentially implies that even if 100% of the portfolio defaulted, principal and interest of this AAA class would not be impaired. It is worth noting that CLO liabilities have historically experienced de minimis default rates. Data from Standard & Poor's shows that from 1994–2013 only eight originally rated investment grade tranches defaulted. This, according to Wells Fargo Securities, represents 0.15% of all investment grade tranches issued in that time frame.

One important feature about CLO liabilities is that they largely ignore the market value of loans. Some financing for high yield debt is based on mark-to-market methodology – a feature that requires margin to be posted at a certain percentage of the market value. The idea for this type of financing is to always maintain a percentage margin of safety. For example, if $1 million of leveraged loans are bought at par (100%) and a 25% margin is required, the financing provider would pay for $750,000 of the purchase price and the buyer would have to pay $250,000. With mark-to-market financing, if the loan price dropped to 90% or $900,000

TABLE 3.2 Sample CLO Structure

	Liabilities				Assets		
Tranche	Rating	Size ($M)	Spread (bps)		Rating	Size ($M)	Spread (bps)
A-1 (60%)	AAA	$300	150		BB	$200	366
A-2 (15%)	AA	75	207		B	200	468
B (5%)	A	25	292		CCC	50	747
C (5%)	BBB	25	360		NR	50	400
D (5%)	BB	25	499		Cash		
E (1%)	B	5	562				
Equity (9%)	NR	45					
	Total Amount ($M)	$500			Total Amount ($M)	$500	
	WA Spread	184 bps			WA Spread	527 bps	
WA Spread	184 bps				Spread Arbitrage	244 bps	
Fees	50 bps				Dollar Arbitrage ($M)	$12.2	
Expenses	7.5 bps						
Credit Costs (1.4% × 30% LGD)	42 bps						
Total Liability Cost	284 bps				Return on Equity	27.1%	

then the financing provider would need its borrowings reduced to \$675,000 (75% of \$900,000). This would require the buyer to increase its investment in the loan from \$250,000 to \$325,000. The concern with mark-to-market financing is that the requirement to post additional collateral in sell-offs can create an environment of forced selling, which precipitates further losses.

CLOs liabilities, in contrast to mark-to-market financings, are long dated and set up to hold loans to maturity. The liabilities do have tests that can require repayment and these primarily relate to collateral coverage. But, importantly, the vast majority of CLOs outstanding have collateral tests that ignore market-pricing fluctuations and instead keep the asset valued at par unless an issuer defaults or the ratings get downgraded below certain pre-determined levels. The CLOs structures are more focused on cash flows and repayment at maturity. The significance of this is that the growth in CLOs, rather than traditional investors that use margin finance, has actually created greater price stability in the leveraged loan market as the vehicles represent "stable hands" – or investment funds that are long-term oriented, committed to the asset class, and less price sensitive.

3.6 IMPLICATIONS OF AN OTC MARKET

Most high yield bonds and leveraged loans trade *over-the-counter* rather than on a national exchange like NASDAQ or the New York Stock Exchange (NYSE). An *OTC market* is characterized as one that exists virtually through a network of trading relationships rather than having a more centrally organized or dedicated physical infrastructure like the NYSE trading floor. There are several reasons why high yield trades OTC including: (1) the relatively smaller size of debt issues, (2) the fact that many issuers do not meet the listing requirements of the exchange, and (3) high yield is more often bought by institutional buyers that do not require an exchange listing to trade. Being an OTC rather than an exchange-listed market has important implications on both market liquidity and transparency.

In an OTC market, broker-dealers such as investment banks serve as market-makers and quote prices where they would buy (*bid*) and sell (*ask* or *offer*) high yield bonds and leveraged loans. If a bond can be bought at 99.5 and sold at 99.75, the bid–ask level is 99.5–99.75. Though these amounts represent percentages, they are commonly stated without the percentage sign. Bid–ask levels in the OTC market are not always firm indications but can just be indicative levels of where a transaction might occur. This is an important difference to more regulated exchange markets. For example, in the case of a NASDAQ exchange-traded stock such as Apple (ticker: AAPL), market-makers are required by the exchange to honor the bid–ask levels. The market-maker must provide liquidity to sellers at the ask price and sell to buyers at the bid price. The OTC market in contrast imposes no such requirements on market–makers. High yield market-makers may stand up to the quote, but most times the bid–ask levels are just a reasonable suggestion of where they think a limited quantity of debt could be sourced or sold. This means that high yield buyers cannot rely on market-makers for liquidity – an important downside consideration. In my experience, buyers must be prepared to hold investments through turbulent market periods because liquidity, as some like to say, is only there when you do not need it.

Though the high yield OTC market is quirky, it actually functions well during normal periods. Every day, dealers distribute thousands of messages or "runs" through mass email and electronic messaging boards. These runs contain information on the bid–ask levels of various high yield bonds and leveraged loans that convey important information on price. The competition for secondary trading revenue keeps many dealers engaged in the market and pricing competitive. For larger $1 billion or greater high yield issues, it is not uncommon to have four or more dealers providing quotes, giving investors multiple options to obtain best execution.

But when markets experience strain, the key differences between the OTC and exchange market manifest themselves quickly. First, high yield dealers have no obligation to make markets in a debt issue, even if it is an offering that they have originated. They often hold little or no exposure in the debt issues, so there is also little alignment with investors. If a dealer becomes more risk-averse, it could either withdraw from market-making, take levels down to facilitate price discovery (and stimulate trading activity), or make "wide" markets, which reflects a growing difference between bid and ask levels (e.g., using our earlier example the bond quote goes from 99.5–99.75 to 98.5–99.5). The bid–ask spread is usually a good measure of market liquidity and pricing efficiency. When spreads are "tight," or within a narrow range, this reflects more efficient trading and accurate pricing. When spreads are wide, this reflects uncertainty on buyer and seller interest – or a growing divide between the two camps.

3.7 TRACKING HIGH YIELD LIQUIDITY

The high yield bond market is tracked by the *Financial Industry Regulatory Authority (FINRA)* through a platform called *TRACE*. Established in July 2002, TRACE (Trade Reporting and Compliance Engine) was developed to facilitate the mandatory reporting of OTC secondary market transactions in eligible investment grade, high yield and convertible bonds. All broker-dealers who are FINRA member firms have an obligation to report related transaction information under an SEC approved set of rules. Since the implementation of TRACE, the reporting time and public dissemination of data has improved dramatically, from 75 minutes to roughly 15 minutes. Investors can utilize this information in their investment analysis for a particular bond or for assessing broader market trends.

Table 3.3 shows how secondary trading volume in the high yield bond market compares with the size of the market tracked by MarketAxess. As shown, secondary trading volume of bonds has not kept pace with market growth. The table shows how turnover, which is defined as the amount of trading volume relative to the market size, has declined in part due to more buy-and-hold investing.

TABLE 3.3   Secondary High Yield Bond Trading Volume Relative to Market Size

Year	High Yield Bonds		
	Traded Volume ($B)	Market Size ($B)	Turnover %
2006	$1,207	$763	158%
2007	$1,060	$743	143%
2008	$1,007	$810	124%
2009	$1,254	$988	127%
2010	$1,284	$1,132	113%
2011	$1,093	$1,048	104%
2012	$1,030	$1,067	97%
2013	$1,033	$1,125	92%
2014	$1,493	$1,516	98%

Source: MarketAxess Corporation

TABLE 3.4   Secondary Leveraged Loan Trading Volume Relative to Market Size

	Leveraged Loans		
Year	Traded Volume ($B)	Market Size ($B)	Turnover %
2006	$325	$313	104%
2007	$526	$499	105%
2008	$507	$576	88%
2009	$470	$563	84%
2010	$413	$511	81%
2011	$409	$509	80%
2012	$396	$524	76%
2013	$517	$598	87%
2014	$628	$755	83%

Source: LSTA Trade Data Study, S&P Capital IQ LCD

The leveraged loan market does not have a regulatory body like FINRA forcing trading reporting by its members. The largest loan market participants, however, have organized through the Loan Syndications and Trading Association (LSTA) to promote a "fair, orderly and efficient" loan market. The LSTA is a valuable source for information and produces studies on market trends. Table 3.4 shows LSTA data on secondary loan trading. The trend with leveraged loans is more prominent – as the investor base has become more institutional, the volume of leveraged loans traded annually has increased significantly. With 83% turnover in 2014 or $628 billion traded in the secondary market, the leveraged loan market is much more liquid than many believe.

3.8   TOTAL RETURN SWAPS AND MARGIN FINANCE

Total return swaps (TRS) and *margin finance* are two ways to finance purchases of leveraged loan and high yield bond purchases. By utilizing lower cost borrowings to buy high yield debt, borrowers can enhance returns on their capital, but they also risk increasing volatility and magnifying losses. A total return swap is often used to finance leveraged loans, because they are not securities that can be bought on margin like stocks or bonds.

Margin finance is commonly employed in stock brokerage accounts, where money can be borrowed against existing holdings to expand portfolio holdings. If the value of the assets in the account decline, the loan obligation must be repaid so that it can maintain a certain loan-to-value (e.g., 50%). In the high yield market, prime brokers, or broker-dealer financing arms, provide this capital to high yield bond buyers and the mechanics work similarly. The amount and cost of financing available usually depends on the client and the collateral. For a large, liquid high yield bond issue the margin requirements can be under 15%. This highlights how efficient the financing market for high yield has become and illustrates the level of comfort prime brokers have with managing bond collateral.

Leveraged loans as we've discussed are not securities and eligible for margin finance. However, this is not to say that they can't be bought with financing. As we discussed earlier, a CLO structure raises liabilities to finance a pool of leverage loans. Some leveraged loan closed-end funds obtain low-cost loans to expand portfolio holdings and enhance expected returns. TRS is another mechanism used to finance loan purchases, more often by hedge funds and large institutions. Similar to margin finance, it is considered a mark-to-market financing that is sensitive to the underlying collateral prices.

The mechanics of TRS financing differ considerably from traditional margin finance but the end result – providing the economic benefit of low-cost borrowings – is the same. In a TRS, the client (often a hedge fund) engages in a swap transaction with a TRS provider. The TRS provider uses its own capital, which it can borrow at low rates being an investment grade entity, and buys the assets that the client seeks to own. This may be an individual loan or bond, or a portfolio. The client, in this case a hedge fund, posts collateral to protect the TRS provider's credit risk associated with this purchase, which is similar to how traditional margin works. All losses become the risk of the client. The rewards, however, are shared – the TRS provider, in this example, charges a set fee for the credit line, usually based on a spread to LIBOR (e.g., 3 month LIBOR + 115 bps) and then pays to the client any residual income or gains from the portfolio.

There are two key differences between TRS and margin finance worth noting. First, the TRS provider owns the assets, becomes the lender of record, and may control voting. The TRS therefore connotes economic benefit to an investment fund rather than control, though this is sometimes circumvented through agreements where the TRS provider agrees to act at the direction of the fund. Second, the rate of interest charged is based on the *notional amount* of debt in the TRS rather than the amount borrowed. For example if a $50 million portfolio of loans is purchased with $15 million of collateral – interest costs of the TRS are based on $50 million of notional even though the TRS provider is only theoretically advancing $35 million, because $15 million of margin has been posted. This makes TRS users sensitive to the amount of collateral required by the TRS – as the interest costs do not decrease if more margin is posted, which stands in marked contrast to how traditional margin finance works.

It is worth noting that not all high yield debt can be financed with margin or TRS and there are no standard eligibility requirements across banks. When considering whether to finance a high yield bond or leveraged loan, prime brokers and TRS providers focus on some combination of: (1) minimum bond or loan size (e.g. $150 million) to ensure sufficient liquidity, (2) the number of broker-dealers quoting the bond/loan, which serves as an imperfect proxy for liquidity, (3) the weighted average ratings of the portfolio or *WARF score*, (4) the amount of *covenant-lite* issuance as a percentage of total, (5) obligor concentration, and (6) industry concentration. When investing with funds that use credit facilities, margin finance or TRS, it's important to understand these parameters and what back-up financing plans the manager has in place.

Understanding how the high yield OTC market functions as well as the drivers of margin finance provides insight to how high yield can perform in stressed environments. In 2008 and 2009, the loss of market-making quotes from Bear Stearns, Lehman Brothers, Merrill Lynch, and Wachovia caused many loans and bonds to be non-compliant with their financing conditions during an unfavorable time to sell assets. The market sell-off during this time period was not, as many believe, triggered by CLOs. One of the key drivers behind the sell-off was mark-to-market financings such as TRS. According to my conversations with industry participants, it has been estimated the market for TRS financing in 2007 was over $125 billion, which represents one-quarter of the leveraged loan market at that time. Not only was mark-to-market financing more prevalent pre-2008, the terms were more aggressive, only requiring 10% margin for certain issues. This, in my opinion, is why the 2008–2009 time period represented the worst stretch of volatility in the high yield market in over 30 years.

TRS financing providers have made important changes to safeguard the industry. The most important is that the terms of TRS financing have become significantly worse for investors. For example, the largest and most liquid high yield loans at the time of writing often require 20%

collateral – double the pre-recessionary levels. This has reduced the levered returns available on loans financed and therefore demand for TRS. At year-end 2014, based on my discussions with leading TRS providers, TRS is an approximately $25–$40 billion industry, roughly one-quarter its pre-recession size. This reduction has occurred while the loan market has grown by approximately 50% in size, implying the influence of TRS on the leveraged loan market is significantly lower today.

3.9 SUMMARY

High yield debt is traded over-the-counter by broker-dealers and is more often purchased by QIBs than individual investors. The buyer base for leveraged loans and high yield bonds varies considerably with investment funds that have differing mandates. Bond buyers have more flexible mandates, evaluating their high yield exposure against other asset classes, while loan investors tend to be more committed to the asset class. This in part relates to the difficulty in financing leveraged loans, which are not securities, as well as differences in the buyer base. With more committed investors, no ability to short sell and higher quality debt, the loan market is inherently more price stable than bonds, though both experienced significant volatility in 2008 in large part due to short-term, price-sensitive financing.

CHAPTER 4

High Yield Financial Concepts

High yield debt has economic features common to other fixed income asset classes. However, its two segments, high yield bonds and leveraged loans, differ in some important ways, which can affect how each performs over time. This is particularly true in changing interest rate environments, where the fixed interest payment structure of bonds more starkly contrasts with the floating rate payment structure of leveraged loans. But it is also true as it relates to call protection, an economic feature of debt that imposes financial penalties on the issuer for early repayment. Differences in the call protection of leveraged loans and bonds affect how each market segment trades in price. To assess the value of high yield debt, it's useful to deconstruct yields and spreads into a risk-free rate and risk premium. The risk premium reflects the compensation provided for risks such as default loss and illiquidity risks, which can be valued in several different ways. This chapter concludes with an overview of financial metrics that can be used to evaluate fundamental risk of issuers such as leverage and interest coverage ratios.

4.1 KEY ECONOMIC TERMS OF HIGH YIELD DEBT

High yield debt shares many common economic features with the broader fixed income market. For example, all debt is issued in an amount that is commonly referred to as the *face amount* or *notional value*. Bonds or loans are sold to investors at a *price*, which can be at *par* (100% of face value) or a value above or below par. When debt is issued at a value below par, the difference is referred to as *original issue discount (OID)*. OID is one way issuers enhance yields on debt offerings. The discount provides more potential for capital appreciation, a form of return. Debt investors make profits not just on interest income but also by price appreciation and fees that can result in the ordinary course, such as a fee a borrower pays to its lenders for early repayment or an amendment to its credit agreement.

Compared to high yield bonds, leveraged loans are more often senior claims with a first right of payment. Loan maturities tend to be shorter, ranging from 5–8 years. Most loans also require periodic repayments prior to maturity. These *prepayments* take several forms and can range from *mandatory amortization* payments (e.g., the issuer must repay 1% of notional per year) to *excess cash flow sweeps* where a certain percentage of the issuer's annual *free cash flow* must reduce the outstanding loan balance.

Bonds, in contrast to loans, generally represent longer term capital to issuers on more flexible terms. Most bonds are issued with a 5–10-year *bullet maturity,* which is when the principal amount of the bond becomes due. Generally an issuer of bonds plans to deploy its cash toward growth initiatives such as funding the expansion of a store base, developing new assets, or acquiring smaller competitors rather than repaying debt. Bond repayments are rarely required prior to maturity. In exchange for providing longer term, fixed rate obligations, which carry more interest rate risk, bond investors seek more duration than loan investors. This means they want their debt outstanding for a longer period of time to ensure a sufficient level of profits. This is accomplished by imposing hefty penalties on issuers for early repayment. Loans in contrast are often match funded, meaning the borrowing costs and term more closely align with the assets, and therefore can be more easily repaid with a lower breakage costs. For example, a loan with interest payments that reset quarterly can be funded by an investor using lower cost, short-term borrowings.

4.2 HIGH YIELD CALL PROTECTION

Call protection, as the name implies, prevents issuers from "calling," or repaying, debt prior to its scheduled maturity date. For investors, it ensures a debt investment offers duration and a minimum amount of profit. Since investors assume the risk that results might deteriorate, in which case the price of the debt will decline, they want some incentive if the business improves. That incentive could be to remain invested at the same interest rate in a company with a lower credit risk. As a company's risks decline, the price of its debt can appreciate to reflect lower risks. When price rises, yields, a measure of return on the investment, decline. Lower yields reflect a lower risk premium that is warranted for a performing credit.

Loans sometimes offer modest call protection, generally allowing an issuer to repay a loan in the first two years at a 1%–2% penalty and at par thereafter. Loan prepayment protection can often be in the form of *hard call* or *soft call* protection. Hard call, as the name implies, offers little flexibility to the issuer around the prepayment penalty. If the call protection is a soft call, then the penalties only apply if the issuer is seeking to refinance the loan with a lower yielding debt rather than in all instances. The idea behind hard and soft call is to distinguish between events where all should benefit (such as the sale of a company that should benefit debt and equity investors) versus opportunistic transactions, like refinancing the loans at a lower rate, which benefit the equity investors but cause lenders to lose an attractive loan or have it repriced. Today, most first lien leveraged loans have no hard call protection and only soft call protection for the first six months to a year after the issuance. Most second lien loans have a modest 1%–2% hard call protection for the first couple of years.

Bond call protection is more onerous to issuers than loan call protection. A 10-year note, for example, generally cannot be repaid for five years. In year five, the issuer can redeem the notes by paying the principal amount owed plus a prepayment premium, which industry convention has set at half the coupon. As an example, a bond with a 10% coupon can be repaid in year five at 105% of its principal value. After year five, the prepayment penalties step down to eventually reach par or 100% one year prior to maturity.

If an issuer wants to redeem its bonds during the non-call period, it would have to pay a *make-whole premium*, which amounts to the present value of all interest payments due through the first call date and includes the prepayment premium. The discount rate is usually equal to the rate of low risk investments readily available for capital redeployment, generally assumed to be equal to the rate of treasury debt with a comparable maturity plus 50 basis points or 0.5% (this discount rate is commonly referred to as T+50). The only exception to prepayment by a make-whole premium would be prepayment in connection with an IPO. Known as an *equity clawback*, most bonds have a provision that allows for the issuer to repay approximately 35%–40% of the bond offering at par plus the coupon (or 110% in our example) with cash proceeds from an equity offering. This equity clawback exception is included in order not to dissuade an issuer from going public and raising equity proceeds, which can de-risk the credit profile. To raise capital through an IPO, an issuer must often commit to reduce its debt with the proceeds.

Call protection allows debt to appreciate to prices well above par when the issuer performs and the required risk premium correspondingly declines. Debt that lacks call protection rarely trades at values more than 1–2 percentage points above par while bonds with call protection can trade at levels above 110%. The significance of this is that bonds that have call protection offer more pricing upside, and therefore capital appreciation potential, than loans. Loans, in contrast, are sometimes price constrained; the risk of a refinancing (which repays the loan at par) prohibits the loan from trading much above par. So even if the loan might warrant a lower yield, which would result from a higher price, it is unable to appreciate. When loans trade above par, it usually represents an opportunity for the borrower to refinance at lower rates – it's a signal to issuers that investors are comfortable lending at a lower rate.

4.3   FIXED VERSUS FLOATING RATE DEBT

High yield bonds and leveraged loans – the two broad market segments – pay interest differently and this affects how each segment performs. High yield bonds, which account for approximately two-thirds of the high yield market, most often have a fixed or set rate of interest. A $500 million debt issue with an 8% interest rate and eight-year maturity is an example of a fixed rate bond. This bond would pay $40 million of interest per year (or 8% multiplied by $500 million) until year eight when all principal is due. *Fixed rate* debt instruments have interest payments that do not change over time. Leveraged loans, which account for the remaining one-third of the high yield market, differ from bonds by having a *floating rate* of interest. Though the benchmark can differ, these loans most often pay interest based on a spread or premium to the London Interbank Offered Rate (LIBOR). Floating rate loans therefore have interest payments that change with LIBOR rates. If a loan has a 3% spread to LIBOR, and LIBOR is 2%, then the loan will pay interest at 5%. If LIBOR increases to 5%, the loan will pay interest at 8%. It should be noted that a small percentage of bonds (particularly secured bonds) do have a floating rate of interest and there are no rules against bonds being structured this way. The high yield bond and leverage loan markets evolved with fixed and floating rate structures in large part due to the needs of their respective investor bases.

TABLE 4.1 Bond and Loan Payments in Changing Interest Rate Environments

	Size	Interest Rate	Current Payment	Payments when Rates Rise / Decline				
				Lower Rates			Higher Rates	
LIBOR		5.00%		2%	4%	5%	8%	10%
High Yield Bond	$250	10.00%	$25	$25	$25	$25	$25	$25
Leveraged Loan	$250	LIBOR + 3.0%	$20	$12.50	$17.50	$20	$27.50	$32.50

High yield bonds and leveraged loans can perform differently in changing rate environments. When rates rise, bond interest payments stay the same while loan interest payments increase, which leads to loans offering greater value to the investor. When rates decline, loan payments decline while bond payments remain constant, which means that the investor holding bonds will be at an advantage to one who holds loans. The hypothetical scenarios listed in Table 4.1, which compares the interest payments from a $250 million 10% bond to a $250 million LIBOR+3.0% leveraged loan, illustrate how these two high yield market segments can present more or less appeal in different interest rate environments. Though the payment on the leveraged loan is initially lower than the bond, it can be greater if LIBOR, which tracks interest rates, increases.

Despite these differences, the high yield market eludes easy generalization on how it will perform in changing rate environments. Bonds for example might offer less value relative to loans in rising rate environments, which could cause them to underperform. But if interest rates rise in response to a fast-growing economic environment, high yield bonds might perform well because the prospects of high yield issuers are improving. When economic and business prospects are good, default expectations decrease, which cause risk premiums to decline. Conversely, if interest rates decrease, bonds with a fixed interest payment offer more value than floating rate loans and can potentially outperform these. This might not be true though if the rate decline reflects poor economic prospects, which might cause bonds to decline in price more rapidly than leveraged loans. The differences between how these two segments of the high yield market will perform in changing rate environments has been further blurred by the introduction of a so-called *LIBOR floor*, or a minimum level of the LIBOR component of the interest rate. For instance, if LIBOR floor equals to 1%, the leveraged loan priced at 3% over LIBOR will never bear interest of less than 4%, even if LIBOR falls down virtually to 0. The key take-away is that high yield debt is not only sensitive to changing interest rates. Because of its "high yield" nature, most issues are insulated from small interest rate changes and more sensitive to changes in the economic outlook, which affect issuer prospects and credit risk premium.

4.4 BOND YIELDS, THE RISK-FREE RATE, AND CREDIT SPREADS

To understand the sensitivity high yield has to interest rate versus credit risk, it's important to look at yields and spreads. Deconstructing yields and spreads into a risk-free and risk-premium component also provides a means to assess potential performance.

A debt's *yield* is its rate of return. The yield is based on the price of the debt, interest rate, and any other economic features. If an investor paid a price of 100% (or par) for a note that pays 10% interest, the yield is 10%. Yields and interest rates differ when the entry and exit prices vary. For example, let's assume the same note could be bought at 90% of par or an investor has to pay $900 for every $1,000 bond. If this bond matured in three years, its yield would be 14.2%. This is because the investor would pay $900, obtain $100 of interest income for three years (or $300) and $1,000 of principal at maturity (or $1,300 in total proceeds). In this example, the yield is greater than the interest rate of the debt instrument because the investor also obtains upside from the note appreciating in value from 90% to 100%.

Some market commentators characterize the high yield asset class as under- or overvalued based on the yield of a high yield index. But how do you know whether a 5% or 10% yield is attractive? Comparing absolute yields over time ignores one critical variable – the *risk-free rate*, which is considered the rate at which the government can borrow. The idea behind the risk-free rate is that if one can invest in U.S. government debt at a certain rate, and that debt is deemed by rating agencies as the safest fixed income investment, then all other U.S. debt must command a premium to that rate – otherwise, why would anyone take the risk of investing in lower quality credit. Risk-free rates set a price floor on borrowing costs.

If the U.S. 10-year Treasury bond is yielding 5%, then lower quality debt issues of comparable term must offer compensation at a higher rate. This excess rate, called the *risk premium*, reflects the compensation provided for the risk of that debt above and beyond the risk of U.S. government debt. Looking at the yield alone, without subtracting the impact of the risk-free rate, says little about the compensation for credit risk.

All yields can be broken down into two components: the risk- free rate and the risk premium. The risk premium is also called the *credit spread* and can be simply understood as the difference between the yield and the risk-free rate. Credit spreads are commonly stated in *basis points* (*bps*) with 100 bps equal to 1.0%. Bonds and leveraged loans use different risk-free rates because of their differing payment structures. Because interest rates are commonly fixed for the life of a bond, the risk-free rate used is the maturity matching Treasury bill. This is often the five-year Treasury bond. Though loan maturities vary, loan spreads are generally based on the three-month LIBOR because loan interest rates are floating and often reset quarterly with LIBOR. To make the risk-free rate and risk premium for bonds and leveraged loans clear by example, if a bond had a 7% yield and the five-year Treasury rate was 2.5%, the risk premium would be 4.5% or 450 bps. If a loan had a 5% yield and the three-month LIBOR rate was 0.5%, the risk premium would also be 4.5% or 450 bps.

Investors look at credit spreads to gain a sense of the potential value from debt. This value reflects the excess compensation being provided for the probability of *default loss* and illiquidity risk, among other factors. Default loss is based on default rates and losses and can be estimated using past experience. If the high yield bond market had a 4% chance of default and an estimated loss of 55% in default scenarios, it would imply the asset class required 110 bps of compensation (4% multiplied by 55%) just to compensate for anticipated default-related losses. But what if the index was priced at a 300 bps spread to the five-year Treasury? This might imply that spreads overly compensate for risks or perhaps the market is factoring in a greater than historical default loss to occur. Another factor that contributes to credit spreads is illiquidity. When investing in government debt, liquidity is less of an issue for most buyers – government debt issues are large and actively traded. However, smaller debt issues with more limited investor bases might prove more illiquid in stressed environments. This lack of liquidity theoretically should provide for some additional compensation, but it is less straightforward to quantify, in part because buyers' needs

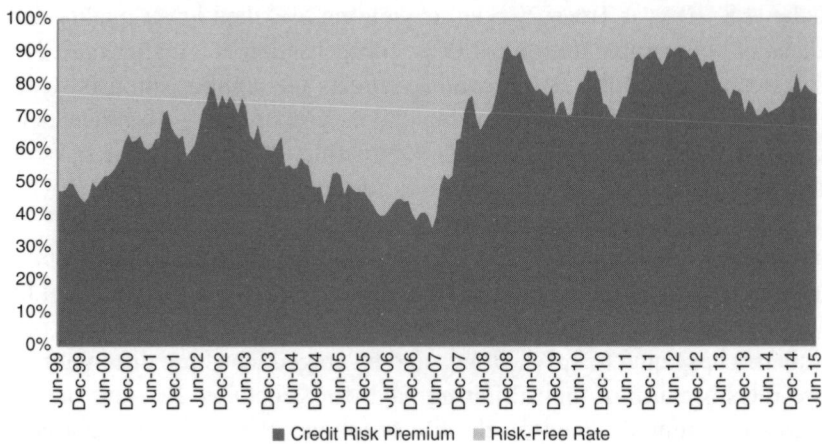

FIGURE 4.1   Risk-Free/Risk Premium Yield Components over Time
Source: J.P. Morgan

with respect to liquidity differ. Understanding spreads is important to fixed income investments and having a view on fair value can provide guideposts on investing. I provide some guidelines to use as it relates to evaluating spreads and liquidity in Chapter 8.

Figure 4.1 shows the percentage of historical yield derived from the risk-free rate versus the risk premium. The best opportunities in high yield are usually found when credit risk premiums increase and represent a disproportionate percentage of the yield. The challenge for investors is that this often happens in environments with greater uncertainty. During these time periods, it's important to understand the nature of the risk. Patient, long-term investors can benefit when spreads widen due to illiquidity risk, which is more technical than fundamental in nature and is something that occurs in flight to quality environments. Default loss risk premium on the other hand relates to more fundamental credit problems and needs to be carefully underwritten.

4.5   MORE ADVANCED YIELD AND SPREAD CONCEPTS

There are several different ways yields are assessed in the high yield market. With leveraged loans, the yield is sometimes calculated with an assumption that the loan is repaid in three or four years from either its

TABLE 4.2 Bond Yields at Varying Prices and Call Dates (10%, 6-Year Note)

Year		3	4	5	6
	Call Premium	105.0%	102.5%	100.0%	100.0%
Purchase Price					
100%	**Yield**	11.5%	10.5%	10.0%	10.0%
95%	**Yield**	13.6%	12.2%	11.4%	11.2%
105%	**Yield**	9.5%	9.0%	8.7%	8.9%

issuance or from its expected duration. This is because few loans actually make it to maturity – most are refinanced or repaid in the years prior to reaching maturity. Thus, if you are buying a loan at a discount to par – let's say 98 – and it ultimately gets repaid at par, the two "points" or 2% (200 bps) of potential capital appreciation has a different impact on yield if it occurs over a shorter versus a longer time period. For example if it occurred over one year, it would add 2% to the yield, if it happened over two years, it would add 1% to the yield. Expectations on when the loan will either get repaid or trade at par are a consideration in an investor's yield projections.

With bonds, the jargon used to express value is complicated not just by pricing discounts or premiums, but also by call protection. As discussed, call protection, which imposes prepayment penalties on the issuer, allows a bond to trade at a premium to par. When looking at a bond's yield, it's important to understand the impact call protection might have. This can be explained more clearly by way of an example. Let's assume a high yield bond with six years until maturity has a 10% interest rate and is non-callable for two years, then pre-payable at 105% in year three, 102.5% in year four, and par thereafter. Shown in Table 4.2, if the bond is purchased at par, it will have a 10% yield at maturity. If the company has underperformed expectations the bond would likely trade at a lower price to provide higher compensation. A price of 95% for example offers investors a higher yield of 11.2%. Conversely, if the company has lowered its credit risk, a lower yield would be justified. At 105%, the yield is 8.9%. Table 4.2 highlights not only the different yields that different purchase prices imply, but how these yields also change depending on when the bond is repaid. An investor interested in this bond would be willing to pay a premium if they believed the company would likely repay this debt in year three or four. During that time period, the yields are higher due to call protection. The point is that when evaluating an investment in this bond, investors will look at a number of different scenarios as call protection affects potential yield.

The three different yield calculations investors focus on are:

- *Yield-to-call* (*YTC*): the YTC is the rate of return an investor would realize if the bond is called by the issuer at the first call date, which in the above example is year three. If the bond, in our example, is bought at 100% and repaid at 105% in year three, it will have an 11.5% YTC.
- *Yield-to-maturity* (*YTM*): the YTM is the return at maturity – in year six using our above example. If a bond was bought at 95% (or $950 per $1,000 face value bond), received 10% interest per year ($100) and was repaid at 100% (or $1,000 per bond) at maturity, it would have an 11.2% YTM. The reason this amount is higher than the interest rate is because the bond is purchased at a discount to the value it is ultimately repaid at.
- *Yield-to-worst* (*YTW*): the YTW tends to be the most commonly used metric by debt investors, who want to underwrite to the worst possible scenario. In the scenario where the bond is purchased at 105%, the YTW is 8.7% in year five. Since this is the worst possible yield based on the bond's call schedule, it is known as the YTW.

These three yield concepts provide a way of comparing bonds against one another. Another yield concept investors consider is *effective yield*, which is often thought of as the *current return*. Effective yield expresses the running rate of return from an investment, ignoring other financial aspects. To calculate the effective yield, divide the annual interest income by the purchase price. Using one of the above examples, dividing the 10% interest rate over the 105% purchase price equates to an effective yield of 9.5%, which is the rate of return absent any price changes or repayment.

4.6 COMMON ISSUER METRICS TRACKED

High yield debt investors are most focused on an issuer's ability to service debt obligations as they become due. In this regard, many debt investors consider a company's ability to generate ample free cash flow (FCF) as the most important consideration when making an investment. Free cash flow is the cash available after all cash obligations are met including interest expense and other fixed charges, taxes, capital expenditures, and working capital needs. It is the amount of cash available for debt repayment or future investment at year-end. Some companies have unfunded obligations like large pension liabilities or other expenses like restructuring costs that deplete FCF. Others have assets like net operating losses which lower taxes and improve FCF. Understanding the sources and uses of an issuer's cash flow is critical to understanding its outlook.

EBITDA is a concept related to FCF and stands for earnings before interest, taxes, depreciation, and amortization. EBITDA is intended to serve as a proxy for the cash flow available to service debt obligations. Depreciation and amortization are added back because they are non-cash charges; incidentally, all other non-cash charges are added back to EBITDA as well, even though this may not be apparent from the abbreviation itself. EBITDA is intended to provide a metric that can be more consistently benchmarked over time and convey a trend of whether or not a company is improving its operating cash flow or debt service capability.

Adjusted EBITDA is a concept that strips out one-time gains and losses from EBITDA. Some companies experience one-time gains or losses that are not indicative of recurring cash flow. Most times these items are commonly accepted "add-backs" or adjustments to EBITDA. EBITDA can also be adjusted for an acquisition made over the prior year, to provide "pro forma" credit as if the acquisition had occurred at the beginning of the period so that EBITDA includes a full 12 months of earnings. EBITDA can also be pro forma for certain cost reduction actions, or the normalization of some event, whether or not any changes have actually taken place. These pro forma adjustments are often not required to be made in accordance with SEC rules (i.e. Article 11 of Regulation S-X). Instead, the calculations simply need to be made in good faith by the issuer, regardless of whether such pro forma adjustments may need to be reflected in pro forma financial statements prepared in accordance with SEC rules. In certain cases an officer's certificate is required and some deals will limit the amount of pro forma cost reductions.

The many versions of EBITDA – from plain vanilla EBITDA to pro forma adjusted EBITDA – highlight its importance to both buyers and investors. It's a metric that affects two key risk metrics – the leverage and interest coverage ratios. The *leverage ratio* conveys information on the quantum of debt relative to cash flow. It ignores the cost of capital and simply focuses on how many times larger the company's debt position is versus its EBITDA. For example, a business with $500 million of debt and $100 million of EBITDA would have "5x leverage ratio" or be

"5x levered." The *interest coverage ratio* focuses instead on the cost of the debt and expresses this cost in relation to EBITDA. If this same company with $100 million of EBITDA had $50 million of interest expense it would have a 2x interest coverage ratio.

Leverage and interest coverage ratios are important metrics to gauge credit risk. Companies in the high yield market are often valued on EBITDA multiples. If a business is estimated to be worth 7x EBITDA and its debt is 6x leveraged (or finances to 6x debt/EBITDA), it suggests the company is highly leveraged and has a low margin of safety. If the debt maturities are near-term, there would be a material refinancing risk and therefore a greater probability of default. If this same company had debt that was 4x leveraged, the debt would seem well protected and relatively low risk. In normal markets, this company would have little difficulty refinancing its debt even if it was coming due.

When looking at leverage ratios, it is important to distinguish between a "total" leverage ratio and "*net*" leverage ratios, i.e., leverage ratio that looks at debt net of cash. Companies with a significant cash accumulation may look very differently when evaluated on the basis of a total leverage and net leverage ratios. However, it's important to keep in mind that cash can be spent and therefore does not necessarily imply a lower future debt liability.

What leverage multiples don't convey is a company's ability to meet its interest expense. Interest coverage ratios, which divide EBITDA by interest expense, state how well the interest expense is covered. The debt that finances LBOs, for example, commonly has a 2–2.5x interest coverage ratio, meaning EBITDA is 2–2.5x larger than interest expense. What interest coverage ratios are supposed to convey is how much room there is for cash flow deterioration before an interest payment would be missed. Another variation of the interest coverage ratio that is helpful to look at is EBITDA minus capital expenditures divided by interest expense. By reducing the numerator by capital expenditures, investors can get to a better proxy for cash flow and a more conservative interest coverage metric. Some capital intensive companies may have good EBITDA/interest expense interest coverage ratios but these may look weak when subtracting capital expenditure requirements. Finally, leverage of companies (such as retailers) that have significant rental costs may be best evaluated on the basis of leverage ratio that accounts for rental expense both in the numerator and denominator, such as debt, plus 7–8x rental expense divided by EBITDA plus rental expense (a concept known as *EBITDAR*).

During hot markets, it's not uncommon to see pricing decline while leverage ratios increase and interest coverage ratios decline. EBITDA adjustments may also increase as issuers market more aggressive transactions. These are all signs of increased risk taking. When leverage declines and interest coverage ratios improve, the market environment suggests more conservative underwriting. EBITDA, leverage, and interest coverage ratios are not perfect but they do provide proxies to track important trends in the marketplace, a topic we discuss in Chapter 8.

4.7 SUMMARY

High yield debt shares many common characteristics with other fixed income obligations. All high yield debt has a yield, which is influenced by economic features such as price, interest rate, maturity, amortization, and call protection. Bonds and leveraged loans have some important distinctions, which allow them to trade differently and also to have varying interest rate sensitivities. There are a number of ways to describe the value of high yield debt including yield-to-maturity, yield-to-worst, and yield-to-call. Deconstructing yields and spreads into a risk-free rate and a risk premium can give insights on the compensation being provided for expected default loss, illiquidity, and other risk factors. Combining an understanding of spreads, which can be driven by the supply and demand of high yield debt issues, along with fundamental trends that can be tracked through credit ratios such as leverage and interest coverage ratios, provides a means to assess asset class value.

CHAPTER 5

Debt Structures

A high yield issuer might have multiple loans and bonds outstanding and these claims can have varying risk based on their claim to collateral and respective seniority. Similar to how capital structures parse out debt and equity risk to buyers with more specific risk-return targets, bonds and loans are structured with differing risk-return attributes. High yield debt structures can range from senior secured loans that are well secured by collateral and carry a low interest rate to holding company notes that offer a double-digit yield as compensation for equity-like risk. The various debt obligations of an issuer carry different risks, which affects not just the expected return of each obligation but also its potential for price volatility.

5.1 RANKING AND SUBORDINATION

Ranking (or *seniority*) and *subordination* are important concepts and the natural starting point for understanding how debt claims differ. Both terms indicate where debt claims stand in relation to each other. In practice, each concept accomplishes the same goal of making one claim more senior to another and for that reason the terms are often used interchangeably. The difference between ranking and subordination is actually more technical in nature, and matters more in downside scenarios, such as one where the issuer underperforms, or in market sell-offs where higher risk assets trade with greater price volatility.

Ranking is a descriptive term that denotes a debt's status. Rank distinctions are made on: (1) whether or not the debt is secured and (2) its level of seniority. All high yield debt can be classified in a binary way as either *secured* or *unsecured*. If a debt is secured, it means that it has a lien on, or security interest in, assets that constitute collateral pledged in support of its claim. If a company is unable to pay its interest expense or debt as it comes due, lenders with secured claims can foreclose and sell this collateral to obtain a recovery. Secured claims therefore have greater credit support than unsecured claims because they benefit from a security interest in the collateral. A detailed description of the relative priority of a bond vis-à-vis other instruments in a capital structure is listed in the "Ranking" section under the Description of Notes in an offering memorandum.

Seniority, which is another descriptive term often included in the name of an instrument itself, relates to an ordering of payments for claims with similar collateral status. If a company has two unsecured bonds outstanding, one bond might be called "senior notes" while the other is called "junior notes." Senior claims, as the term suggests, get repaid prior to junior claims. To ensure they get repaid first, senior debt claims generally have maturities inside of junior claims. The longer duration of junior claims, along with their less senior positioning in the capital structure, results in junior debt having higher risk and a higher interest rate relative to senior debt.

Combining these concepts, the highest priority debt claims in a capital structure are ones that are *senior secured*. Senior secured debt benefits from liens on assets and payment seniority over other debt claims. Over 90% of the leveraged loans that are included in major indices are senior secured claims.[1] In the high yield bond market, there has been a growing trend toward senior secured notes issuance, but this category of debt still represents less than 25% of outstanding bond issuance.[2] The majority of high yield bonds are senior unsecured notes, which means they are unsecured obligations with a senior payment status.

Subordination is a legal term that describes the interrelationship, or relative priority, among various tranches of debt. High yield debt has three types of subordination: (1) *payment subordination*, (2) *lien subordination* and (3) *structural subordination*. The difference between each of these types of subordination is more significant in downside scenarios, such as bankruptcy, but the gist of each type of subordination is the same as ranking in making one class of debt explicitly more senior in payment priority. In the event of a foreclosure or distribution in bankruptcy, subordination creates

---

[1]S&P Capital IQ LCD (S&P LSTA Leveraged Loan Index).
[2]BofA Merrill Lynch Global Research (BofA Merrill Lynch US High Yield Master II Index).

a waterfall, pursuant to which a more junior debt can only be paid after a more senior debt is paid in full.

Payment subordination is most relevant to senior subordinated notes, the third largest class of high yield bonds. A senior subordinated note ranks junior to any senior debt claims, including senior notes and senior secured loans. If the issuer is performing, interest is paid to all claims in the ordinary course when due and the subordination provisions never come into play. However, if the issuer defaults on a senior debt claim by not making an interest payment, interest payments on subordinated notes will be automatically blocked. Furthermore, if the issuer breaches any covenant contained in the senior debt, the senior debt holders may issue a *payment blockage notice* to the subordinated noteholders to "block" interest payments. The payments on junior debt are blocked to limit the amount of assets such as cash that are distributed to junior claims. When important assets included in the collateral that might constitute a downside recovery are distributed to junior claims, this is often referred to as *collateral leakage*.

The payment block arising out of the non-payment of interest on a senior debt can be permanent, whereas payment blocks arising out of the covenant breaches cannot occur indefinitely. After 180 days (the period of a semi-annual interest payment), the senior subordinated noteholders can *accelerate* – or declare their debt due and payable – if the interest payment has not been made.

Another important feature of payment subordination, which is rarely used in the high yield bond market but is very popular in a privately issued high yield debt (also known as mezzanine debt), is a *remedies block*. Generally, when a debt claim is accelerated, or declared due and payable before its maturity date, it precipitates a restructuring that often requires Chapter 11 to resolve. To avoid allowing junior debtholders to force the hand of senior debtholders in a restructuring scenario, the junior debt may be subject to a remedies block or *standstill*, which prevents junior debtholders from accelerating their debt for a certain period of time ranging from 90 days to 180 days, unless the senior debt has been accelerated first.

Lien subordination occurs with secured claims and therefore is more often a provision related to leveraged loans. The largest market segment subject to lien subordination is *second lien loans,* which in 2014 was a $43 billion asset class, representing roughly 5% of outstanding leveraged loans.[3] Second lien loans maintain a security interest in the company's

---

[3]S&P Capital IQ LCD.

collateral but that lien is subordinated to the lien held by the *first lien* term loan. Most liens are perfected security interests enforceable by law. When a company has two loans outstanding with varying lien priority, the loans are usually referred to as a first lien and a second lien loan to distinguish their security interest.

It is important to understand that both first and second lien loans are senior loans with respect to payments. In other words, while second lien loans may not receive proceeds from collateral until the first lien loans are paid in full, the second lien lenders can recover from any other assets not classified as collateral without regard to the payment of the first lien loans. While as a practical matter, both first and second lien loans are secured by substantially all assets of the company, there are always exceptions and those exceptions can constitute an important source of recovery for the second lien lenders. Another major difference between lien and payment subordination is that lien subordination payments to a junior or second lien holder cannot be blocked by the senior or first lien holder. Only debt that is explicitly subordinated can have its payment blocked by another lender. Thus, lien subordination is often preferred by investors to payment subordination, as when a company is underperforming it might result in an additional interest payment, which could constitute important recovery.

5.2 OPERATING AND HOLDING COMPANIES

Prior to addressing structural subordination, it's helpful to understand the corporate organizational structure of high yield issuers. Most high yield issuers are organized with several operating subsidiaries and then legal entities that group these entities together, known as holding companies. Operating subsidiaries are the entities that are engaged in business activities and generally where the assets reside. For example, if a company sells widgets in Mexico, China and the United States, it might operate subsidiaries – or separate legal entities – in each of these geographies for tax, regulatory, and accounting purposes. If this company wanted to borrow capital, it could potentially raise capital at one of these legal entities.

Holding companies generally have no business activities and exist only to own operating subsidiaries. This same company that sells widgets in three geographies would have a holding company that owns its three operating subsidiaries. The holding company owns the equity of operating subsidiaries; it therefore has ownership and control of those legal entities. If this company wanted to borrow debt against all its operations rather

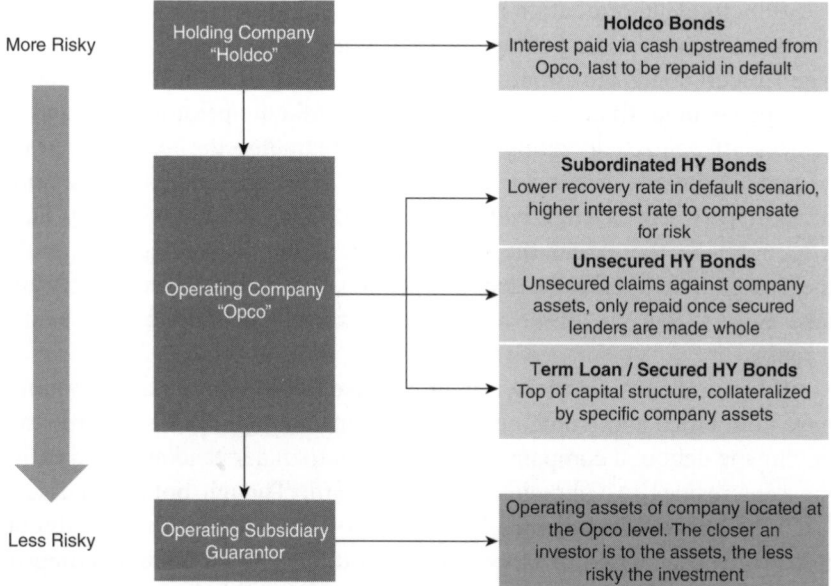

FIGURE 5.1 Capital Structure with Opco and Holdco Debt Obligations

than from just one operating subsidiary, it could raise debt at the holding company. If the debt was *guaranteed* by the operating subsidiaries – a legal term meaning that the operating subsidiary is legally obligated to use its assets to service that debt – then the debt would have a direct claim on the operating subsidiary's assets just as if it resided at that entity.

To benefit from the assets of the entire operation, high yield debt is often issued by a holding company that owns the equity of operating subsidiaries. This gets complicated when various levels of holding companies exist. As it relates to high yield issuers, the holding company that owns the equity of operating subsidiaries and benefits from guarantees is referred to as the *operating company* or *Opco*. The holding company that owns the equity of Opco is known as the *holding company* or *Holdco*. Holdco's only asset is the equity of Opco, while the Opco has the equity of operating subsidiaries and guarantees. Therefore any claims at Opco are more senior to claims at Holdco.

Leveraged loans and high yield bonds are usually issued at the Opco level. High yield issuers sometimes also issue debt at the Holdco level. Figure 5.1 illustrates a more complex capital structure with debt claims at both the Opco and Holdco levels.

Structural subordination refers to debt that is junior because it resides at a more remote holding company, such as the Holdco bonds in Figure 5.1. The Holdco bonds are structurally subordinated to debt at Opco, whereas the Opco debt is structurally subordinated to debt at operating subsidiaries (unless, of course, operating subsidiaries guarantee the Opco debt thus becoming directly liable for it, in which case structural subordination of the Opco debt is effectively eliminated). The Holdco will only have a recovery to the extent the Opco retains equity value. For this to be the case, all of the Opco debt claims must be satisfied in full. A key take-away is that the closer a debt claim is to the assets the more senior it ranks.

Structural considerations matter because large high yield issuers often have both Opco and Holdco debt claims outstanding. For credit investors buying the debt of a company, it is important to understand at which entity the debt resides to appreciate its risk-reward. Though both debt issues might be called "senior notes," a senior Holdco note has a very different risk profile than a senior Opco note. It is only with an understanding of ranking, subordination, and how Opco and Holdco debt differs, that the different types of debt structures that manifest themselves in the high yield market become easier to understand.

5.3 LEVERAGED LOAN STRUCTURES

Over 90% of leveraged loans have a first priority lien and are known as "first lien loans."[4] This means they are usually entitled to repayment before any other debt claims in the capital structure including unsecured obligations incurred in the ordinary course of business such as accounts payable. First lien loans are primarily floating rate loans, though nothing precludes them from having a fixed rate (it is just very rare). The loans are generally issued at an Opco that is guaranteed by substantially all operating subsidiaries. Because of their senior status in the capital structure, first lien loans tend to have more polar outcomes in default scenarios, with the majority achieving a full recovery and a smaller percentage incurring catastrophic losses – where only limited recovery is possible. To provide some sense of performance, over the past 17 years approximately 3.4%

---

[4]S&P Capital IQ LCD (S&P LSTA Leveraged Loan Index).

of outstanding first lien loans have defaulted per annum.[5] On average, recoveries, or the amount of the claim unimpaired, have averaged 68% on first lien loans during default situations.[6] This highlights how, over time, the vast majority of first lien loans have been money-good.

Revolving credit facilities and *asset based loans* (*ABLs*) are two different types of capital lines that provide the issuer with the flexibility to draw-down and repay capital based on its needs. The facilities are committed to by lenders and carry a small unused, commitment fee. When the company draws on this capital, the borrowings are made at a stated interest rate until they are repaid. In a sense, revolving credit facilities operate very much like credit cards under which a company can borrow, repay, and re-borrow within its credit limits. Revolving credit facilities are generally *pari passu* with the company's first lien term loan obligations and therefore carry a similar rate of interest.

ABLs are a type of revolving credit facility that provide capital based on an advance rate against certain assets, such as accounts receivable and inventory. The amount available from an ABL is sized by the quantification of the issuer's current assets, with some haircut, to provide for greater asset coverage. This amount is called a *borrowing base*. A typical ABL facility will have a borrowing base capped at the amount equal to 85% of the value of accounts receivable and 65% of the book value of inventory (or 85% of the net liquidation value of the inventory). The percentages – called advance rates – may differ depending on the lenders' view of the quality of current assets. Low quality receivables and aged inventory may be ineligible for inclusion in the borrowing base. As these assets move up and down in value, so can the amount of potential ABL borrowings. Because ABLs are secured – in fact, oversecured, due to the haircuts imposed by the advance rates – by specific, more liquid (and therefore realizable) assets, they tend to be low cost for issuers.

ABLs will always have a first priority security interest in the current assets which comprise their borrowing base but are often subordinate to the secured term loans on other assets. It is not unusual for a large high yield issuer to have an ABL revolver, a first lien term loan, a second lien term loan, and, sometimes, even senior unsecured bonds. In this situation,

---

[5]Moody's Investors Service and J.P. Morgan – "J.P. Morgan High Yield Default Monitor – June 2015."
[6]J.P. Morgan; Moody's Investor Service.

the intercreditor arrangements and relative ranking become particularly important in evaluating the potential risk of each instrument.

Second lien loans are a relatively new class of debt, with the structure starting to gain popularity in the early 2000s. Second lien loans, as the name suggests, are a junior form of secured debt. They are repaid after first lien loans but ahead of unsecured obligations such as senior notes. Initially, second liens were issued by smaller companies, who could sell first lien debt more efficiently through syndicated offerings but historically had to rely on *private placements* of junior debt due to their limited size, which made them illiquid and less desirable to most high yield investors. The growth in second liens has occurred as non-bank investors with more ability to buy illiquid debt offerings have taken a greater share of the leveraged loan market. CLOs and hedge funds, for instance, can buy second lien loans with less concern about liquidity risk. The growth in second liens not only reflects changes in the investor base for leveraged loans but also the increased willingness of high yield investors to buy smaller syndicated issues.

Because of their smaller, less liquid size and junior collateral status, second liens are usually priced at a premium to comparably rated bonds. This is also due to the fact that second liens, unlike bonds, are not securities that can be easily margin financed and therefore must offer higher unlevered yields. For issuers, second lien loans provide two key benefits. First, compared to the alternative of privately placed debt, which is typically held by one or at most a few parties, the cost is usually lower due to its appeal to a broader group of investors who also benefit by having some liquidity. Second, as compared to bonds, second lien loans have less onerous call protection. A company that is high growth, cash-flow generative, or seeking to make transformative acquisitions or a near-term exit, might derive significant value from the more flexible call features of second lien debt, which often permits the second lien loans to be redeemed at relatively low premiums, such as 102% in year 1, 101% in year 2, and at par thereafter.

The newness of second liens makes it somewhat of an unproven asset class with limited historical performance data that can be relied on. Of course, the idea of debt secured by a subordinated lien is nothing new; it's just that we haven't yet gathered enough default and recovery data on the asset class to quantify its risk with any degree of accuracy. As a result, this type of loan is more questionable and has both its advocates and critics. Advocates for second lien debt believe that the compensation provided for the risk is significant and adequately compensates the investor for the risk being assumed. They also argue that the loans are less volatile than comparably rated bonds due to their inability to be traditionally shorted, as well as their limited size, which can create a more stable investor base. Critics, in turn, point to the often weak documentation protections of second lien loans and the potential for low recoveries in downside scenarios. The truth in my experience is that the second lien market is difficult to generalize due to the wide range of companies issuing loans and the differences in risk and holders across issues. In my view it is simply a market segment with a greater degree of idiosyncratic risk.

A *unitranche* is a type of loan popular with small to mid-sized companies. In this type of financing, a lender provides one loan that encompasses both the senior and junior debt risk instead of parsing it up. For example, if a company with $30 million of EBITDA could raise $100 million of first lien debt and $50 million of second lien debt through a syndicated offering, the unitranche equivalent would be a single tranche that is $150 million in size. The rate of this debt would be somewhat comparable to the blended average of the first lien and second lien loans. Middle-market direct lenders are increasingly providing unitranches to differentiate their capital from what is available in the syndicated capital markets. Traditional investors in syndicated loans, such as banks and CLOs, tend to be more ratings driven and generally prefer higher quality first lien loans and potential small investments in second lien loans. Direct lenders, such as private debt funds, are less focused on ratings and more concerned with risk-return.

The benefit of unitranches to issuers is that cash flow pays down debt at its average cost. This stands in contrast to a traditional first and second lien loan structure (or first lien/bond structure), where cash flow pays down first lien debt first, which is lower cost than second lien debt. The unitranche therefore allows for greater interest cost savings over time. Another benefit for issuers is that private investors in a unitranche can move quickly, provide certainty, and may be less difficult to work with for the amendments or modifications that are often required in the ordinary course.

The downside for issuers using a unitranche is the risk of being beholden to one or a handful of lenders who might prove unreasonable and difficult to work with. The other concern for issuers may be the opaqueness of a unitranche as unitranche lenders of record often "unwind" the structure on the back end by slicing and dicing the blended rate to different sub-lenders. In addition, when credit market conditions improve, it's more difficult to refinance a unitranche loan at lower rates versus a syndicated offering with its greater pool of potential lenders who can be played off each other in order to secure the best possible terms.

5.4   HIGH YIELD BOND STRUCTURES

The senior note is the most common high yield bond. Senior notes are generally issued at the Opco or entity where the leveraged loans are raised, and ranks similarly in seniority status. However, because senior notes are unsecured, they are considered junior claims to first and second lien loans and rank *pari passu* or equivalent to other unsecured obligations of the Opco including unsecured accounts payable. In the ordinary course, the ranking of this debt has no practical implications. However, in downside scenarios, where the issuer defaults on an interest payment and cannot repay all its debt, seniority status matters more.

In 2014, there were over 1,730 senior notes issues accounting for approximately $1 trillion of debt.[7] At its current size, senior notes represent 75% of all high yield bonds outstanding and therefore most funds that provide high yield exposure are usually invested in these notes.[8] Given its lengthy history, there is substantial performance data available on senior notes. Similar to first lien leveraged loans; senior notes have averaged a mid 3% default rate over the past two decades. However, because of their more junior positioning in the capital structure, the average recovery of senior notes has been lower than first lien loans and has been approximately 40%.[9] Most bonds perform well, but the range of outcomes for underperformers is more disparate, which allows for greater trading volatility.

Senior subordinated notes is a class of debt prevalent in more highly leveraged and complex capital structures, where an issuer raises loans, senior notes, and then this more junior type of debt obligation. Senior subordinated notes are debt claims at the Opco but junior in right of payment to any first and second lien loans as well as to senior notes. The term "subordinated" makes it a junior obligation and actually allows for more senior creditors to block payments to the senior subordinated noteholders, whose cash might prove to be an important recovery in downside scenarios. Post the Great Recession, the use of senior subordinated debt has declined considerably to the point where senior subordinated notes were close to non-existent in 2015. This volume trend, depicted in Figure 5.2, reflects the lack of large-cap buyouts, which necessitated large debt financings

---

[7]BofA Merrill Lynch Global Research (BofA Merrill Lynch US High Yield Master II Index).
[8]Bank of America Merrill Lynch Global Research.
[9]Moody's Investors Service and J.P. Morgan – "J.P. Morgan High Yield Default Monitor – June 2015."

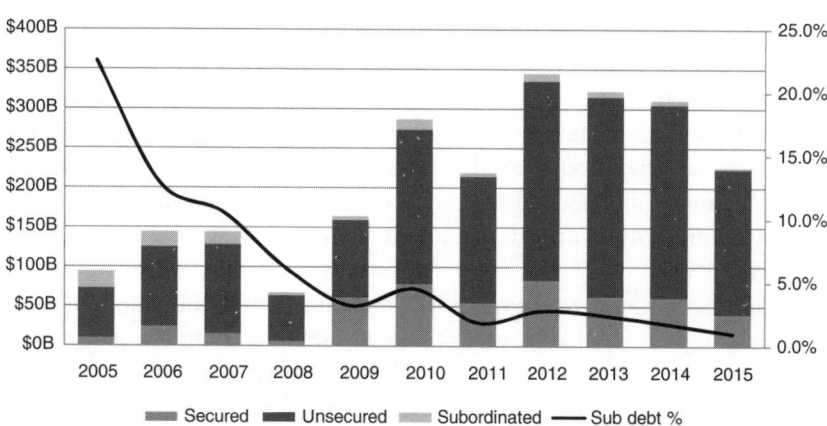

FIGURE 5.2 High Yield Bond Issuance by Debt Type
Note: As of September 30, 2015
Source: S&P Capital IQ LCD

with many ranking tiers, that the market experienced pre-recession. It also reflects the growing role of first lien and senior notes in a capital structure, which today are providing more leverage and eliminating the position that senior subordinated notes once held.

Senior secured notes represent a relatively small portion of high yield bonds outstanding but their use has grown. In recent years, 20%–30% of new issuance has been in the form of this type of bond, as shown in Figure 5.2. A senior secured note is the bond version of a unitranche, where the bond encompasses both the risk of senior and junior debt. For example, if a company could raise $200 million of first lien debt and $150 million of bonds, it might instead raise $350 million of senior secured bonds. Issuers who are too small to issue a bond alongside a first lien loan often use senior secured bonds. When bond offerings are too small, or less than $200–$250 million, they often command premium pricing due to their relative illiquidity. Investors generally prefer to invest in larger bond issues that have multiple investors and are traded more actively. A senior secured note accomplishes that goal and can provide access to the bond market at more efficient pricing. Senior secured notes often have a first lien on certain collateral and a second lien on other collateral such as accounts receivable. Companies that issue senior secured notes, also require revolving credit facilities, which serve as working capital lines or capital that can be drawn down for smaller acquisitions or investments. These loans, which are intended to be more short term in nature, are often structured as first-out facilities, i.e., while they have the same priority claim on assets as senior secured bonds, they are paid first in the case of a default or bankruptcy of the issuer. Also if the issuer owns a significant pool of current assets (such as inventory and receivables), these revolving loans may be structured as ABLs, having a first priority security interest in current assets and second priority security interest in other assets. The latter structure is more prevalent with retailers and can be useful in meeting seasonal needs.

Holding company notes are most often senior note obligations of the holding company. Unlike leveraged loans, senior secured bonds, senior notes, or senior subordinated notes, holding company notes do not benefit from operating subsidiary guarantees. The holding company's only asset is the equity of Opco. Holding companies are essentially shell companies with no business operations. The purpose of this structure is to allow issuers to raise debt that is junior to all Opco liabilities but senior to the equity. Because of their junior payment status, holding company notes have limited rights and their payments can be cut-off by Opco creditors without this leading to a default. In default scenarios, the outcome for holding company notes tends to be binary. For this reason, and because interest cannot always be serviced in cash, holding company debt usually offers a high double-digit rate of return. The interest rate is often tiered, where it can be paid at a lower rate if it is paid in cash and a higher rate if it is paid through additional debt claims, a concept known as payment-in-kind (PIK). Many Holdco bonds are structured with a 75 bps premium for PIK (e.g., 10.5% interest rate if paid in cash, 11.25% interest rate if PIK). The concept of payment-in-kind debt is discussed in more detail in the following section.

Most holding company notes are raised by issuers who use the proceeds to provide a distribution to its owners. When a company is performing, its lenders often seek opportunities to provide it with more capital. Owners can take advantage of this dynamic and use markets where there is limited high yield new issuance and strong demand to lock-in a return on their equity investment. The rate of return on this debt is less than the expected return on equity and its interest can be tax-deductible, subject to the AHYDO rules discussed below. Holding company notes are a risky form of investment, particularly when interest is paid-in-kind rather than in cash. Cash interest serves as a form of recovery and de-risking. With holding company notes, lenders are essentially providing senior equity without any control. It is an aggressive structure that is usually a signal of enhanced risk-taking in the marketplace.

5.5 PAYMENT-IN-KIND DEBT

Sometimes the interest rate of a high yield bond or loan can be paid through additional debt claims rather than cash. This type of interest payment is called *payment-in-kind (PIK)*. If the interest is PIK, the lenders' claim will increase at the rate of interest. As an example, a $300 million 10% PIK bond would provide lenders with $15 million of additional debt claims at the first semi-annual interest payment date. The bond size would increase to $315 million with all lenders earning an increase proportionate to their debt holdings. At the next interest payment date, the issuer would have to make a semi-annual payment of $15.75 million to account for this higher debt balance. PIK debt tends to result from situations where a cash payment is prohibited by more senior debt claims or the issuer needs relief from cash interest payments because it is growing or recovering from a setback such as bankruptcy. PIK structures were particularly popular in the mega-buyouts of the early 2000s and during the period leading up to the Great Recession. Those bonds had a *PIK toggle* feature, which allowed the issuer to pay a lower interest rate in cash or pay a higher interest rate in additional debt. Though PIK structures have grown in popularity, today they represent a small portion of the market. The structure must be viewed cautiously because without interest payments, the investment does not offer a return until principal is repaid.

5.6 AHYDO

Debt which pays interest at high rates and PIKs for significant periods caught the attention of Congress, which introduced special rules related to *applicable high yield discount obligations* into the tax code, commonly known as *AHYDO*. Congress' objective was to defer or disallow tax deductions for interest on debt that resembled equity finance. Some high yield debt instruments fall within the ambit of the AHYDO rules.

From an issuer or investor's point of view, first it's important to know that AHYDO issues will most likely arise in high yield bonds that pay interest in the form of additional debt (such as PIK instruments) and have a maturity of more than five years. Second, in order to prevent debt from being subject to the AHYDO rules, issuers often introduce bonds into an AHYDO catch-up payment feature, which requires the issuer to repay in cash the portion of the additional PIK debt that exceeds federally allowable amounts on the first interest payment date after the fifth year anniversary of the issuance of the bonds. The AHYDO prepayment is usually made at par, notwithstanding the otherwise applicable call premium and, therefore, should be taken into account when evaluating the return on the bonds. AHYDO is a more technical area of high yield finance, but one worth flagging as it is consequential for investors and issuers who are contemplating PIK debt.

5.7 SUMMARY

High yield issuers often have complex capital structures that span various types of high yield debt at Opco and Holdco levels. While debt claims can share the same issuer risk, differences in rank and subordination can alter the risk-reward and trading volatility of individual issues. There are many types of leveraged loans and bonds outstanding. The most common leveraged loans have a first lien on collateral and are generally the first debt to be repaid. The most common bonds are senior unsecured notes, which are situated between a company's loans and equity in terms of payment priority. Tracking trends in new issuance, a topic covered in Chapter 8, can provide insights on underwriting standards and market conditions. Certain types of debt claims, such as Holdco notes and PIK debt, can constitute more aggressive financing structures common when market conditions are more issuer friendly as the result of demand for high yield debt exceeding supply.

CHAPTER 6

Credit Agreements and Legal Considerations

This chapter introduces high yield credit agreements. Bond and leveraged loan credit agreements are set up to provide issuers with flexibility to conduct their operations while providing lenders with an important voice on matters related to collateral protection. The outline of a high yield bond and leveraged loan credit agreement are similar but contain some differences, particularly as it relates to covenants. Covenants outline the obligations an issuer agrees to abide by in order to protect collateral value for the lenders. In the process of explaining how credit agreements are setup, this chapter provides insight on the most important provisions of the credit agreement and an explanation, in simple terms, of commonly misunderstood industry jargon such as maintenance covenants and covenant-lite. It also discusses recent legislation including the Volker Rule and its impact on the high yield market following the Great Recession.

6.1 LOAN CREDIT AGREEMENTS AND BOND INDENTURES

In industry terminology, leveraged loans are governed by *credit agreements* and bonds by *indentures*. A loan credit agreement and bond indenture are both legal contracts that outline the key economic terms, issuer representations, covenants, default provisions, and voting rights that govern a high yield debt instrument. Investors and issuers negotiate the terms of these documents using specialist corporate lawyers and investment bankers as intermediaries. Many high yield document provisions that address administrative details employ commonly accepted market standards and clauses. We refer to these, effectively "boilerplate" provisions, as the "plumbing" of the document. Some *covenants*, or provisions that impose obligations or limitations on the borrower, tend to involve more intense negotiations, particularly as they relate to situations where the interests between equity owners and creditors can diverge. An example of this is if a company wants to raise more debt capital to fund growth opportunities. Lenders might be wary of additional claims on the collateral, particularly as there is a risk that the investment does not actually lead to growth. To protect against this scenario, lenders could impose restrictions, through covenants in the credit agreement, which only allow the issuer to borrow additional debt capital if it is performing to certain standards.

To understand the differences between loan and bond credit agreements, it's important to keep in mind the traditional buyers of each asset class. Leveraged loans were originally held by relationship banks. These banks made relatively low-cost borrowings secured by the best assets and structured credit agreements that were fairly restrictive in order to protect their interests. The theory was that if the company needed more flexibility than these agreements provided, the company could work with its relationship bank on a reasonable solution that met the needs of both groups. A borrower could more easily accept the potential risk that the parties would not arrive at a solution because loans can be repaid with low breakage costs. Therefore, if the relationship bank proved unreasonable, the issuer could, at least in theory, find another lender to do business with.

The bond market developed to a lesser extent by way of relationship lending and more by way of the pooling of institutional buyers to buy new issues. Bonds, as we explained in Chapter 4, have more call protection than loans, which means that they are more costly to repay early. If an issuer needs more flexibility than its bond indenture provides, it has more limited negotiating power with creditors because of the high breakage costs. Also, bonds are generally more junior claims than leveraged loans in the capital structure. For these reasons, bond indentures have historically offered more flexibility to issuers than leveraged loan credit agreements. This being said, even though a bondholder doesn't have a voice on issues that pertain to an issuer's loans, they do indirectly benefit from the more restrictive terms contained in the credit agreement.

6.2 ROADMAP TO HIGH YIELD DOCUMENTATION

A sample table of contents for a bond indenture and leveraged loan credit agreement are listed below in Table 6.1. Though these documents seek to enforce similar protections, they are structured slightly differently and can be confusing given the amount of industry and legal jargon used. A proper explanation of these provisions could be the subject of its own book and, candidly, is more information than is required for individuals familiarizing themselves with the asset class. What is more important to understand regarding high yield credit agreements is the substance of these provisions and what they allow for and prohibit.

While the number of Articles and Sections may vary from deal to deal, they are all broken down by similar topics. A bond indenture is often organized into 11 articles. Article 2 deals with legal and administrative issues, such as defining certain terms in the agreement and detailing mechanisms

TABLE 6.1 Table of Contents of a Bond Indenture and Leveraged Loan Credit Agreement

	Bond Indenture		Leveraged Loan Credit Agreement
Article 1	Definitions and Incorporation by Reference	Section 1	Definitions
Article 2	The Securities	Section 2	Amount and Terms of Commitments
Article 3	Redemption	Section 3	Yield Protection
Article 4	Covenants	Section 4	Representations and Warranties
Article 5	Successor	Section 5	Conditions Precedent
Article 6	Defaults and Remedies	Section 6	Affirmative Covenants
Article 7	Trustee	Section 7	Negative Covenants
Article 8	Discharge of Indenture	Section 8	Events of Default
Article 9	Amendments and Waivers	Section 9	Administrative Agent
Article 10	Guarantees	Section 10	Guarantees
Article 11	Miscellaneous	Section 11	Miscellaneous

for issuing, paying, and cancelling notes. These are important details, but can be viewed as more closely connected to the "plumbing". Article 3, which addresses "Redemption", outlines the call protection of the notes, which can be a significant source underlying the economics of high yield bonds, as discussed in Chapter 4. The guts of the indenture are in Article 4, which outlines covenants. Article 5, entitled "Successor," limits the ability of the issuer to merge or sell all or substantially all of its assets. "Defaults and Remedies," Article 6, outlines what constitutes a breach of agreement and allows the lenders to accelerate their claims, or declare the bonds due and payable. Articles 8 through 11 are more "plumbing," relating to topics including the duties of the trustee, the mechanisms for amending the credit agreement, the guarantees in place, and other housekeeping related items that address a wide range of scenarios.

The typical credit agreement is broken down in 11 main categories although the number of sections may vary. Compared to the bond indenture, there are several overlapping topics such as Definitions, Covenants, Defaults and Miscellaneous. Further, Section 2, "Amount and Terms of Commitments" covers the same topic addressed in "The Securities" of the indenture. However, unlike bonds, leveraged loans are typically floating rate based. Section 3 addresses yield protection issues. Section 9, "Administrative Agent," highlights a key difference between bonds and loans. Leveraged loans are administered by an administrative agent, which is usually an arranging bank that takes on the responsibilities of facilitating interactions between the issuers and investors. Administrative agents normally have a lot of discretion and will drive the negotiations of the terms of credit agreements. Bondholders instead rely on a trustee, whose role is largely ministerial and who lacks any discretion whatsoever. The difference between the roles of trustees and administrative agents also explains why bond indentures tend to be more loosely structured than credit agreements. Since bonds are traded in book-entry form, mostly through Depository Trust Company (DTC), Euroclear and Clearstream (for European issues), the identity of actual bondholders is hard to ascertain. As a result of the trustee's inability to make discretionary decisions and the difficulty in ascertaining beneficial holders of bonds, it is practically impossible to negotiate any amendments to a bond indenture outside of the public consent solicitation process.

Another category that differentiates credit agreements from bond indentures is "Representations and Warranties," or Section 4, which ensure full disclosure of information about the issuer to the investors. As such, they exist only in the context of the leveraged loans, since high bonds as securities are subject to rigorous disclosure requirements, which allow investors to rely on the disclosure contained in the offering document.

The main difference between the credit agreement and indenture relates to covenants. The difference is not so much related to bonds' combining affirmative and negative covenants in one article (Article 4) and then singling out the merger covenant in a separate Article (Article 5), while leveraged loans break covenants into affirmative and negative (Sections 6 and 7). Rather the difference, as discussed in the following pages, is in the substance of the covenants in each document. It should be noted, however, that with the convergence of the high yield markets where more and more traditional bond purchasers purchase leverage loans and vice versa, this difference has been slowly eroding and in some transactions, has all but disappeared in favor of looser, bond-like covenants.

You have probably noticed that the description just provided omitted any mention of Article 1, which contains defined terms. Since the provisions of high yield documents are long and verbose, drafters tend to simplify them by combining many details into defined terms that are then used in a capitalized format in operative provisions. For instance, covenants may permit "the consummation of the Specified Transactions if the Specified Transaction Conditions are satisfied." Unless you review the defined terms, you will never know which transactions are permitted by this clause and what are the relevant conditions to their consummation. In fact, many important rights and flexibilities of an issuer are "hidden" in the definitions Article. Even if you see a familiar term, such as EBITDA, don't assume that it is used in its conventional sense. Chances are it is carefully defined in Article 1 and this definition may make an otherwise familiar concept mean something quite different, which, very clearly, has important implications for the potential investor.

6.3 AFFIRMATIVE AND NEGATIVE COVENANTS

If the word "covenant" brings to memory Cecil B. DeMille's masterpiece, *The Ten Commandments*, with Charlton Heston, as Moses, coming down Mount Sinai with the Tablets of the Covenant, you have a pretty good sense of what the covenants are. (Incidentally, our English colleagues call them "undertakings" in their documentation, which somewhat softens the solemnity of the term.) Covenants are the obligations of the issuer to either do or not do some action. Covenants can be broken down into two categories: affirmative covenants and negative covenants.

Affirmative covenants outline actions an issuer must take in the ordinary course, such as comply with laws, pay taxes, maintain insurance, provide certain financial information, and maintain books and records. While most of these provisions are common across issuers, an affirmative covenant that can vary and is important to investors is the one that imposes reporting requirements on the issuer. Investors want to stay abreast of the issuer's financial position, such that they can periodically re-evaluate their investment. High yield bonds traditionally provide the SEC-required information (whether or not the issuer is a publicly listed company), such as annual, quarterly, and special reports. Leveraged loans also require delivery to the lenders of certain non-public information, such as projections and budgets. Since the receipt of non-public information can bar an investor from trading in public securities of the issuer, the leveraged loans usually provide a choice on whether this information should be provided or not. An investor may designate itself as a "public" lender, who will receive only information that would otherwise have been publicly available or is not forward looking in nature. Or a lender could designate itself as "private" and would receive both public and non-public information including budgets and projections. Being private is preferable because it provides more information on the issuer. However, some organizations prefer to stay public to avoid any conflicts that could result from receiving private and forward-looking information even if the issuer has no public equity.

Negative covenants are key provisions in both credit agreements and bond indentures. Their purpose is to impose restrictions on corporate actions that can adversely affect collateral that support a debt claim. For example, negative covenants can prohibit an underperforming issuer from selling key assets like an overseas operation and using the proceeds to make a distribution to owners. They can also limit the amount of additional debt raised that can prime existing claims or share collateral. The purpose of negative covenants are to scrutinize areas like asset sales, additional debt incurrence, grant of liens, distributions, investments, and transactions with affiliates such as owners. These provisions are negotiated to provide the issuer with flexibility to operate the business yet protect the lenders from actions that will result in a diminution of collateral value.

Negative covenants vary based on where the claim sits in the capital structure. As one can imagine, secured high yield lenders will be much more focused on the preservation of their collateral and may have a somewhat higher tolerance for the incurrence of junior unsecured debt, whereas unsecured high yield lenders will try to make sure that they are not being pushed down the capital structure as a result of the company incurring significant additional secured debt. When investors analyze a high yield investment, they must carefully review the negative covenants to understand what type of flexibility the issuer has to take actions that might benefit the shareholders at the expense of the creditors.

6.4 INCURRENCE-BASED VERSUS MAINTENANCE COVENANTS

There are two types of negative covenants: incurrence-based covenants and maintenance covenants. *Incurrence-based covenants* are incorporated in bond indentures and are only tested when an action is taken. For example, if a borrower wants to incur new debt, liens, sell assets, merge, or take a distribution it must be in compliance with restrictions outlined in the negative covenants related to each of these actions. Sometimes this restriction might state that the company's interest coverage, or EBITDA divided by its interest expense, must be 2.0x pro forma the transaction taking place. The goals of these covenants are not to entirely impede business flexibility but to ensure that the debt claims have sufficient coverage post any transaction that is potentially value detracting. Credit agreements sometimes also carry another form of protection called *maintenance covenants* or *financial covenants*, which is absent in almost all bond indentures. Maintenance covenants impose an ongoing obligation on the issuer to demonstrate its financial health. Common maintenance tests seen in credit agreements include:

- Total leverage ratio or the ratio of total funded debt to EBITDA.
- Senior leverage ratio or the ratio of senior secured funded debt to EBITDA.
- Net senior or net total leverage ratios, which are the same ratios as senior and total leverage ratios, respectively, except that the numerator is reduced by the amount of cash on hand.
- Interest coverage ratio or the ratio of EBITDA to interest expense.
- Fixed charge coverage ratio or the ratio of EBITDA to fixed charges, which may include debt service, dividends on senior equity, and cash

taxes. Furthermore, the numerator may sometimes be reduced by the amount of capital expenditures.

Maintenance covenants are usually measured quarterly on the basis of a trailing 12 months EBITDA. Generally speaking, EBITDA is the most important concept in maintenance (as well as in the incurrence) covenants and should be closely examined. While most are familiar with the conventional definition of EBITDA – earnings before interest, taxes, depreciation, and amortization – the EBITDA definition (see our note above regarding the definitions section) in the high yield documents can run for pages and contain many additional adjustments that would allow the issuer to use a much higher number than the one achieved by using conventional definition. First, EBITDA used in high yield documents is usually a so-called "normalized" EBITDA, i.e., it excludes all extraordinary and non-recurring items. Second, EBITDA is determined on a "pro forma basis," which means, for example, that it will give credit to a full year of credit for the incremental EBITDA of a business that may have been acquired only in the last quarter and will often permit the issuer to add back prospective cost savings and synergies that are expected to be realized but have not yet been realized. Because of such a liberal definition of EBITDA, investors are sometimes surprised that the issuer reports full compliance with the covenants, while their internal calculations show a very different picture.

Maintenance covenants should be viewed as an early warning system as well as a re-pricing mechanism. If the issuer struggles to meet its financial covenants, this is a sign to investors that "something is rotten in the Kingdom of Denmark." The maintenance covenant forces all parties to the table and provides an opportunity for lenders to get better explanations on the source of underperformance and management's plans to remediate the situation. At this point, the investors can take another look at the high yield instrument they own and determine whether they want to continue with this particular investment or require the issuer to pay them off, even if that might entail a loss (the idea being that withdrawal at this stage is preferable to a downside scenario). The mechanism that allows them such a re-assessment is called "events of default" and the related remedy of acceleration, or declaring liabilities due and payable. The threat of default and acceleration is what forces borrowers to cooperate with lenders and take the steps necessary to maintain their support.

6.5 COVENANT-LITE – WHAT DOES IT MEAN?

In recent periods, the term covenant-lite has garnered much attention. Some think that covenant-lite means that the credit agreement lacks any covenants. What covenant-lite refers to are high yield term loans that don't have maintenance covenant tests and therefore only have incurrence-based negative covenants. These credit agreements therefore more closely resemble bond indentures with various protections through representations and warranties, affirmative covenants and negative covenants. A growing percentage of loans are structured as covenant-lite. In 2013, over 57% of leveraged loans issued in the primary market were covenant-lite, compared to 0% 10 years ago, according to S&P Capital IQ LCD.

All things being equal, having maintenance covenants as an investor is better, but that is a simplistic view. With maintenance covenants, what matters is where the tests are set – do they provide an early seat at the table? Over time, the definitions of EBITDA have grown more liberal, allowing issuers to add back and adjust upward EBITDA to higher levels, and the tests themselves have been set at levels so wide, or such as can be cured with capital contributions known as *EBITDA cures,* that the issuer is more likely to have an interest payment default before it has a covenant default. When I was structuring private high yield transactions in the early 2000s period this was not the case. But as the high yield market has grown in size and liquidity, issuers have been able to get better terms on covenants. The transition to covenant-lite or bond-like documentation has occurred in part because maintenance tests had become less meaningful and the leveraged loan market became more liquid.

In my opinion, the growth in covenant-lite is a development in the leveraged loan industry consistent with the transition from a relationship buyer to an institutional buyer base. Maintenance covenants primarily provide an opportunity to re-price an underperforming loan. If a company breaches its covenants, lenders usually waive the covenants for a period of time in exchange for fees and a higher interest rate, along with other limitations that act as austerity measures. Before loans became more liquid and traded as an asset class, maintenance tests helped compensate for illiquidity risk by providing relationship banks with an opportunity to re-price risk if performance at the company deteriorated. Loan investors today have greater ability to sell underperforming positions and therefore rely less on covenants to manage illiquidity risk and downside scenarios.

The data on whether maintenance covenants or covenant-lite loans have had lower defaults or improved recoveries is inconclusive. On the one hand, maintenance covenants can provide an early seat at the table and possibly allow lenders to force changes at a company, changes that might possibly preserve collateral. On the other hand, breached maintenance tests usually impose hefty financial burdens on issuers that are already experiencing strain to meet debt obligations. This can precipitate a downward spiral effectuated in part by the need for consensus, which can result in "lowest common denominator" type of negotiations.

There is an interesting and, almost paradoxical, evidence of practical utility of covenant-lite loans that should be pointed out. As described below in this chapter, federal regulators did not share the same optimistic view of covenant-lite loans. In a traditional heavy-handed fashion, the regulators all but made covenant-lite a curse word. Yet, covenant-lite loans are still alive and well and covenant-lite transactions continue to be brought to the market with a fair degree of regularity. Whether or not such a resilience of this asset class is indicative of its market value is for the readers to decide.

One thing we see clearly though is that maintenance covenants do not necessarily make for a safer investment. Today, it is often the issuer with the more challenging prospects that must offer maintenance covenants in its credit agreement to attract lenders to invest. Higher quality companies more often can raise debt without maintenance covenants because their credit prospects are attractive. When choosing between credit quality and document considerations, the credit in most cases matters more.

6.6 MORE ADVANCED CREDIT AGREEMENT PROVISIONS

While an investment decision is generally made based on the financial attractiveness of a particular instrument, high yield investors review credit documentation to ascertain scenarios including: (1) how much debt the issuer can incur in total and that can rank senior to the contemplated investment; (2) how much value can be siphoned from the issuer by means of dividends or investments; and (3) to what extent the issuer is permitted to transact business with its affiliates not on an arm's length basis (which also has a potential of diminishing business value). Many investors create a checklist that allows them to quickly review credit documents to evaluate the strength of the covenants. This checklist would look at the following provisions listed under negative covenants:

Baskets – baskets refer to exceptions to negative covenants. For example, a company might have a $100 million basket to raise additional debt but otherwise be prohibited from doing so. Baskets are often limited by a dollar amount or pro forma ratio, which essentially means that they are a test that ensures that post the transaction (in this case a $100 million debt raise) the borrower can meet some financial metric. A common ratio used to ensure covenant compliance is an interest coverage ratio of 2:1. If the interest coverage test could be met following the $100 million additional debt raise, it would be allowed. It is important to note, baskets that are not subject to a ratio test potentially constitute means for the borrower to raise more senior capital when it's underperforming. The amounts of these baskets must be carefully considered as they can prime existing claims, which might happen in a stressed scenario when recoveries are more called into question.

Carve-outs – while used interchangeably with baskets, carve-outs more often denote exceptions from negative covenants that are not limited by an amount or ratio but by the type of transactions carved out. For instance, sales of inventory in the ordinary course of business, payments of customary directors' fees, or entering into cash pooling/cash management arrangements are permitted without any dollar limit, so long as a particular activity fits into the conditions delineated by a specific carve-out.

Building baskets – are baskets that "build" over the years by the percentage of cumulative net income or cash flow earned by the issuer. The amount accumulated in a building basket can only be used if the issuer could "incur $1 of debt," and still be in compliance with a ratio test such as the 2:1 interest coverage ratio. *Grower baskets* refer to the baskets that are limited by the greater of a dollar amount and a percentage of total assets (or, sometimes percentage of tangible assets or consolidated annual EBITDA).

Debt incurrence – refers to the ability of the issuer to incur more debt. *Ratio debt* describes a debt basket that is not limited by a dollar amount but rather is subject to a certain financial ratio, most commonly an interest coverage ratio in bond indentures or a leverage ratio in credit agreements. For example, a credit agreement might allow an issuer to raise more debt if it was no more than 5x leveraged (or Total Debt / EBITDA was less than or equal to 5x) pro forma the debt raise.

Layering – refers to the incurrence of debt that would rank senior to the debt purported to be protected by the covenants. Layering is also referred to as *priming*. When this occurs, the risk of an existing investment increases because it becomes a more junior claim. Debt that is layered or primed will often trade down in price or lose value.

Restricted payments – can account for many types of payments that essentially represent collateral leakage. In the context of leveraged loans, it may refer only to dividends and distributions to equity holders, whereas in high yield bonds and some credit agreements, restricted payments can also include prepayments of junior debt and certain investments that would otherwise be restricted. Dividends to owners, which create no economic benefit to creditors, are governed by restricted payments baskets.

Permitted acquisitions – describe the ability of the issuer to grow by buying additional businesses. Oftentimes, the amount of acquisitions that can be made and financed with debt capital is capped and subject to a basket or ratio test.

Restricted subsidiary – denotes a subsidiary that is subject to covenants. Not every restricted subsidiary guarantees the debt. The distinction is important in downside scenarios as other more junior debt claims may have a *pari passu* interest in non-guarantor restricted subsidiaries.

Unrestricted subsidiary – describes a subsidiary that is not subject to the covenants and is free to operate without regard to the restrictions imposed by the high yield indenture. An unrestricted subsidiary might distribute its earnings to the issuing entity to support debt claims. However, it has no contractual obligation to do so. Further, an unrestricted subsidiary could be spun out or distributed to owners without any consideration provided to lenders if it is not part of the restricted group.

While these provisions comprise a list of important negative covenants most investors will seek to understand prior to investing in an individual issue, there are a few other important provisions in the credit agreement and the indenture that investors also pay close attention to. These provisions include:

Additional debt – This section commonly refers to the accordion or incremental facilities in the context of leveraged loans or additional notes in the context of high yield bonds. Traditionally, the high yield bonds indenture has always been an "open" indenture, i.e., so long as the issuer is permitted to incur debt under the covenants described below, that debt may be incurred under the same indenture. Conversely, the leveraged loan agreements permit only a limited amount of debt to be incurred under the same instrument, as lenders are more concerned with collateral sharing issues. Lately, however, the accordions in leveraged loan facilities tend to utilize the bonds approach: if the issuer can incur debt under the covenants, this debt may be incurred under the same credit agreement.

Fungibility – One of the key issues of investing in additional debt is its fungibility with the previously issued tranches. If the additional debt is smaller and not fungible with the original issue, it could trade at a higher premium to reflect greater illiquidity risk or less ability to buy with financing. Fungibility analysis is complex and tax-driven but the outcome is easy to determine. Additional debt is considered fungible with the previously issued debt if it bears the same CUSIP number.[1] If additional debt is issued under a different CUSIP number it may not be fungible with the tranches bearing different CUSIP numbers and, therefore, its liquidity may be impaired.

Most-favored nations (MFN) clause – An interesting feature of additional debt worth noting is the so-called MFN clause. Appearing exclusively in leveraged loans, the MFN clause provides that, to the extent the new debt carries a yield that exceeds the yield on the original tranche by more than a certain cushion, usually 25–50 bps, the yield on the original tranche is increased to maintain

---

[1] An identification **number** assigned to all stocks and registered bonds. The Committee on Uniform Securities Identification Procedures (CUSIP) oversees the entire CUSIP system.

the same cushion. MFN clauses often have "sunset" provisions by which the MFN is automatically terminated after a certain period of time, anywhere between 6 and 18 months after the issuance of the original tranche. In an increasing rate environment, investors are often focused on the duration of the MFN clauses. For instance, in the fall of 2014, when one of the Federal Reserve Board members hinted that it may consider raising interest rates at some point, the investors began demanding MFN clauses of longer duration, sometimes eliminating sunset provisions altogether.

Transferability – While high yield bonds are freely transferable, subject to compliance with the securities laws, leveraged loans are transferable (or, more precisely, "assignable") only with the consent of the issuer and the administrative agent of the loan facility. While the transfer provisions are designed to make loan assignments relatively easy by prohibiting issuers and agents from unreasonably withholding consent, as a practical matter, the assignment of a loan can sometimes take place quite a long time after a trade has been agreed to. To address these inefficiencies, the loan market developed another method of transferring the economic ownership of a loan without the need for issuer consent. If a sale needs to be effected quickly or the issuer consent is not likely to be obtained, a lender of record may sell a "participation" in the loan, as the result of which, a selling lender remains a lender of record but the economic ownership has been effectively transferred to a participant. The obvious drawbacks of this otherwise very efficient method of loan trading are limited voting rights of a participant under a specific credit agreement and a risk that the lender of record files for bankruptcy and the participation will be mired in a bankruptcy process (which was addressed surprisingly efficiently and relatively painlessly in the famous Lehmann bankruptcy).

Change of control – A change of control provision triggers a full repayment of debt upon the change of ownership of or control over the issuer. In a bond indenture, a change of control usually creates a put right, i.e., investors are permitted to require the issuer to repurchase their bonds usually with a 1% premium. In credit agreements, a change of control is usually an event of default that results in the acceleration of the debt. Change of control provisions, especially in the context of a proxy fight or hostile takeover, have lately come under judicial scrutiny as provisions that unduly restrict equity holders' rights to express their views and, therefore, constitute a breach of fiduciary duty by the issuer's board of directors. While the jury is still out (literally) on the fate of the change of control provisions, most likely the definitions of change of control will stay at least in some deals, albeit in an abridged form.

Events of default – Credit agreements and bond indentures are nothing more than contracts between the issuer and its debt holders. As such, as is the case with any other contract, a breach of an indenture or a credit agreement results in investors being entitled to exercise their contractual remedies. However, unlike an ordinary contract, where the parties need to identify the breach and demonstrate damages, debt instruments contain in them both the list of breaches as well as the type of remedies available to the investors. The list of breaches of debt contract are called events of default and the remedies include acceleration, foreclosure (in the case of secured debt), and sometimes the imposition of a penalty interest called default interest. Events of default usually include failure to make payments on the debt, failure to comply with covenants, inaccuracy of representations and warranties (in credit agreements), change of control (in credit agreements), bankruptcy of the issuer, undischarged judgments, and cross-default (or its variation, cross-acceleration). The last one is particularly interesting because in the cross-default situation, the high yield issue performs just fine but some other debt over a certain threshold has entered default, which causes this issue to be in default. Similarly, the default arising out of an unpaid judgment also triggers remedies where the issuer is in full compliance with its debt instrument. So far, both undischarged judgment default and cross-default provisions have been accepted by the issuers and have not been scrutinized by the courts, apparently because market participants understand that investors need protection against this systemic failure.

6.7 SACRED RIGHTS AND BANKRUPTCY RESOLUTION

When a company experiences a *technical default*, which is a non-monetary default such as a covenant breach, resolution is usually reached between the borrower and its lenders. When a company experiences a *payment default*, meaning the issuer does not have the ability to service its debt obligations, a restructuring is usually required. In a restructuring, debt claims are often *impaired*, which means they receive less value than the amount of their principal. The equity investor often loses control of the company to its lenders and its equity stake becomes worthless. Lenders that have value will seek to convert their claims into new debt instruments and possibly equity ownership, which provides an upside if the business recovers.

The challenge with facilitating consensual restructurings is that every lender needs to agree to the terms of the restructuring. U.S. commercial code stipulates that all lenders are afforded certain fundamental rights, which are often referred to as *sacred rights*. Sacred rights relate to actions that cannot be taken without unanimous consent. The four sacred rights are: reducing interest rates, extending the maturity, releasing liens, and reducing the amount of loans. If a restructuring plan was agreed to by all but one lender and it violated a sacred right, it would be prohibited by law. Sometimes this happens because a distressed investor buys a small position in a capital structure that is intended to provide "hold-up value."

Bankruptcy provides a means to break the logjam created by hold-outs or creditors at odds with each other on a resolution. In bankruptcy, a court adjudicates the case, hearing arguments from various stakeholders. The most important rule of bankruptcy is that for a court to approve a restructuring plan and override an investor's sacred rights, the plan must be accepted by one-half in amount and two-thirds in number of the senior-most claim that is impaired. The idea is that if a sufficient percentage of the claim represented by both notional amount and number of investors agree that the plan makes sense, the court will move it forward. Compared to most other jurisdictions, the bankruptcy process in the United States is well tested and generally run by the book. As a result, high yield debt claims can trade with greater efficiency in downside scenarios.

Bankruptcy can be very expensive and damaging to issuers but can also be rehabilitating, allowing issuers to lower debt burdens, shed unprofitable operations, exit over-priced leases, and clear outstanding litigation. The two types of corporate bankruptcies are Chapter 11 and Chapter 7. Chapter 11 restructures a business as an ongoing concern while Chapter 7 liquidates assets and the business ceases to exist. *Distressed investors* often seek to buy high yield debt issues for companies undergoing or expected to undergo a restructuring. When investing in distressed debt, investors must sometimes be prepared to provide the company with more capital in order to support its recovery and strike a deal with other stakeholders.

6.8 RECENT LEGISLATION

A number of laws and regulations that affect high yield debt were developed in response to the Great Recession. In a sense, the years leading up to the Great Recession were largely reminiscent of the "Roaring Twenties" with all its glamour and excesses. Wall Street was booming; new exotic financial instruments were in vogue and attracted enormous amounts of capital. In 2008, the music stopped with the Lehman Brothers bankruptcy, the largest bankruptcy ever known to the financial industry. It became clear that due to the lack of robust oversight, many investment banks were able to leverage themselves to staggering levels and were willing to experiment with the most aggressive products of dubious quality. As the financial industry was poised for a worldwide crash, the government embarked on a bailout program, unprecedented in its size and scope. *Too Big to Fail* by Andrew Ross Sorkin,[2] provides a good description of the events leading to the crisis and the steps taken by the government to avert a complete systemic meltdown.

The system was ultimately saved at a staggering price tag to governments and taxpayers, but when the dust settled, the financial industry landscape changed forever. Most of the major players in the investment banking industry became federally regulated bank holding companies, which made them subject to an increased level of oversight and ultimately forced them to implement more rigorous underwriting standards. In July 2010, the Dodd–Frank Wall Street Reform and Consumer Protection Act was signed into law by President Obama. While not aimed specifically at the high yield industry, the Dodd–Frank Act, as it came to be known, had a profound effect on almost every part of the nation's, indeed, the world's, financial services industry. The Act gave additional powers to the existing regulators and created a host of new agencies, such as the Financial Stability Oversight Council, the Office of Financial Research, and the Bureau of Consumer Financial Protection. More and more market participants became subject to government oversight. The effects of Dodd–Frank rippled through the financial system and, in the words of Barney Frank who co-wrote the legislation, had a "restraining effect" on bank risk-taking.

Section 619 of the Dodd–Frank Act, commonly known as the Volcker Rule (named after its most vocal advocate, the former Federal Reserve

---

[2]Sorkin, Andrew Ross, *Too Big to Fail*. Viking Press, 2009.

chairman Paul Volcker and the advisor to President Obama) deserves a special mention, however, as it significantly curtails the potential for abuses by the investment banks. In a nutshell, the Volcker Rule bars banks from speculating with their own money, prohibits a banking entity from sponsoring an investment fund, and imposes additional restrictions on affiliate transactions. When the rule was still in the works, it was feared that the restrictions on proprietary trading would negatively affect market liquidity by stifling investment banks' market-making activities. Legislation has resulted in primary dealers significantly reducing the amount of corporate debt held on their books.

But of all the legislative developments, *The Interagency Guidance on Leveraged Lending* published by the Federal Reserve, Federal Deposit Insurance Corporation (FDIC), and the Office of the Comptroller of the Currency (OCC) on March 22, 2013 has probably had the most direct impact on the high yield market. The purpose of the *Guidance* was to reduce the number of highly leveraged transactions where the issuer is very unlikely to repay its high yield debt and must rely on its refinancing. The *Guidance* described which loans will be considered non-pass by the Agencies.

The initial reaction by the high yield market participants was not what the Agencies expected. Frustrated by the lack of an anticipated effect on the high yield market, the Agencies published *Guidance FAQ* on November 7, 2014. While the *Guidance FAQ* clarified that no one single factor will result in a leverage loan being assigned a non-pass rating, the Agencies also made it clear that loans with the total debt to EBITDA ratio of 6x or more will raise concerns for most industries. Another factor considered in rating a loan non-pass would be the inability of the issuer to fully amortize all of its senior secured debt or repay 50% of total debt over five to seven years. Finally, covenant-lite loans were mentioned as a potential red flag for the regulators.

In response to the *Guidance*, investment banks have adopted their own internal underwriting standards, which in some cases have resulted in banks passing on lucrative mandates that they viewed as highly leveraged. While the *Guidance* focused on leveraged loans, according to a *Wall Street Journal* article published on December 11, 2014, the banks are not likely to be permitted to skirt the *Guidance* by doing all bond deals because the *Guidance* may not permit any bridge loans required in any committed high yield bond financing. Although the *Guidance* does not have the same sweeping system-wide implications as the Dodd–Frank Act, from a high yield investor's standpoint, the *Guidance* may have improved the quality and risk profile of the asset class.

In the aftermath of the systemic failure of 2008 and the Great Recession that followed, the government signaled a clear trend toward a closer oversight and more pro-active regulation of the financial services industry and financial markets. While such an environment of overregulation may have stifling effects on the markets in the long run, the empirical evidence shows that the high yield market has actually improved as a result. Tighter underwriting standards and more responsible lending has increased investor confidence, which ultimately contributed to the robustness of the high yield market as a whole in the post recession years.

6.9 SUMMARY

Credit agreements and bond indentures outline economic terms and covenants that affect credit risk. While many contract provisions are standard, negative covenants are more extensively negotiated as they govern corporate actions that can diminish collateral, alter the debt's position in the capital structure and divert cash flow to competing stakeholders. Bond indentures have incurrence-based covenants, which mean that the covenant is only tested when a specific action is taken. Loan credit agreements sometimes have maintenance covenants, which are quarterly tests that assess the health of the borrower and can be used to re-price risk if the issuer underperforms. The trend in covenant-lite loans has made credit agreements more closely resemble bond indentures and reflects the growth in institutional loan trading. Document protections ultimately matter when issuers pursue aggressive transactions or encounter duress and need to restructure liabilities. Though consensual restructurings are possible, sacred rights often create logjams which only a bankruptcy process can resolve.

CHAPTER 7

High Yield Asset Class Performance

C hapter 7 delves into how the high yield asset class has performed over time, addressing important topics including returns, volatility, interest rate sensitivity, and default rates. The chapter includes a significant amount of historical performance data on the high yield bond and leveraged loan market that can later serve as helpful reference material. When looking at information produced from high yield market indices, it's important to keep in mind that the index is composed of many individual debt claims whose performance can vary meaningfully over the same time period. Different high yield market segments, whether it is bonds or loans or debt by different ratings category, can under- or outperform depending on economic conditions. Understanding how high yield debt can perform in changing interest rate and economic environments is therefore helpful to assessing the prospects of the market and different investment strategies employed.

7.1 TOTAL RETURNS, VOLATILITY, AND THE SHARPE RATIO

Total returns, volatility, and the Sharpe ratio are three metrics commonly used to measure asset class performance. A *total return*, as the name suggests, reflects all economic gains and losses from the asset. For high yield debt, the total return includes interest income, fees, prepayment premiums, price appreciation/depreciation, and realized gains/losses. To estimate total returns on the high yield market, data is collected on the performance of thousands of high yield debt claims. Major investment banks including Credit Suisse, Bank of America Merrill Lynch, Barclays, J.P. Morgan, and Citigroup employ large teams to aggregate this data and produce proprietary total return indices. In addition, there are more independent research firms such as Standard & Poor's that produce excellent coverage of the market. Total return indices are produced for both high yield bonds and leveraged loans. This data can be analyzed to produce more in-depth studies such as how the debt of a certain rating, seniority, or industry group has performed relative to other market segments.

Volatility is a measure of risk that is based on total return deviations from a mean return. Volatility essentially provides insight on the variability of returns. As an example, if Bond A and Bond B both have an average annual return of 8% over three years, Bond A would be less volatile with returns of 7%, 8%, and 9% compared to Bond B's returns of 16%, –3%, and 11%, A highly volatile asset class can produce a high rate of return one year and a negative return the next; a less volatile asset class is one with a narrower band of outcomes, closer to the mean return. This might imply less upside potential for returns but also less downside risk.

It's important to highlight that the risk measured by volatility is not necessarily related to the fundamental risk of the issuer, whose prospects are more affected by the quality of the management team, competitive advantage, and industry trends among other factors. In theory, fundamental risk and return risk are tied. For example, a more stable issuer should deliver returns more evenly (or with low volatility) while a high risk issuer, such as an exploration and production energy company, might have great results in one year, poor results in the next, and this would manifest in more volatile annualized total return performance. But volatility can also be driven by technical trends in the marketplace such as the supply and demand for high yield debt. Over shorter time horizons, market technicals can overwhelm fundamentals and add or reduce pricing volatility.

The *Sharpe ratio* is helpful for comparing total returns against volatility; it's a measure of risk-adjusted returns. The Sharpe ratio is calculated by taking the annualized total return of a risky asset in excess of the risk-free rate and then dividing this amount by the volatility or standard deviation of returns. The Sharpe ratio strips out the risk-free rate to focus on the risk premium, or excess compensation being provided by the risky asset. It then divides this value by the risky asset's volatility to provide a metric of the return provided for the risk. The higher the Sharpe ratio the better – it means more return for the risk. Sharpe ratios are often used to compare asset classes or fund managers against each other.

7.2 COMPARATIVE ASSET CLASS PERFORMANCE

Total returns, volatility, and risk-adjusted returns provide a common language to compare high yield debt to other asset classes. Table 7.1 shows the performance of the S&P LSTA Leveraged Loan Index (leveraged loans) and the JPM High Yield Bond Index (high yield bonds) against other asset classes from 2000–2014 (excluding 2008). This time period is significant because it includes two recessions, several periods of above-average volatility, and encompasses a period of unprecedented growth in the size of the high yield market. High yield's appeal to investors is readily apparent from this data. The total return from high yield bonds has been higher than returns from the S&P 500 with lower volatility. The leveraged loan asset class has produced high risk-adjusted returns and is further distinguished by having only one negative total return year in over two decades (2008). The high interest income from high yield debt helps offset default-related

TABLE 7.1 Historical Asset Class Performance: 2000–2014

Asset Class	Average Return*	Standard Deviation**	Return / Risk	No. of Positive Years	No. of Negative Years
Leveraged Loans	8.0%	4.7%	1.70	14	0
High Yield Bonds	10.9%	7.4%	1.47	13	1
High Grade Bonds	7.7%	4.6%	1.69	13	1
10-year Treasury	5.1%	7.2%	0.71	12	2
S&P 500	8.1%	14.3%	0.56	11	3

Note: As of December 31, 2014. *Based on monthly return data. **Annualized returns divided by the annualized standard deviation of return. Excludes 2008, a year of exceptional volatility.

Data Source: S&P Capital IQ LCD (Leveraged Loans), J.P. Morgan (High Yield Bonds, High Grade, 10-year Treasury), FactSet (S&P 500)

loss and pricing declines and makes total returns less dependent on capital appreciation.

7.3 ANNUAL PERFORMANCE VARIATIONS

A more granular look at total returns provides insight on how high yield has performed during periods of economic growth, recessions, and changing rate environments. Table 7.2 details the total return performance of leverage

TABLE 7.2   Historical Asset Class Performance and Macro Metrics

	Asset Class Indices – Total Return					Macro Metrics	
Year	Leveraged Loans	High Yield Bonds	High Grade Bonds	10-year Treasury	S&P 500	U.S. GDP	10-year Treasury Yield
2014	1.6%	2.2%	7.8%	10.9%	13.7%	2.4%	2.2%
2013	5.3%	8.2%	−0.8%	−7.7%	32.4%	1.5%	3.0%
2012	9.7%	15.4%	9.9%	4.2%	16.0%	2.2%	1.8%
2011	1.5%	7.0%	8.7%	17.0%	2.1%	1.6%	1.9%
2010	10.1%	14.7%	9.3%	8.3%	15.1%	2.5%	3.3%
2009	51.6%	58.2%	18.5%	−8.8%	26.5%	−2.8%	3.9%
2008	−29.1%	−26.6%	0.5%	20.2%	−37.0%	−0.3%	2.3%
2007	2.0%	2.6%	6.0%	9.8%	5.5%	1.8%	4.0%
2006	6.8%	11.6%	3.8%	1.4%	15.8%	2.7%	4.7%
2005	5.1%	2.4%	1.4%	1.9%	4.9%	3.3%	4.4%
2004	5.2%	11.1%	6.0%	4.7%	10.9%	3.8%	4.2%
2003	10.0%	26.8%	8.2%	1.7%	28.7%	2.8%	4.3%
2002	1.9%	3.2%	10.7%	14.6%	−22.1%	1.8%	3.8%
2001	4.2%	6.7%	10.7%	3.7%	−11.9%	1.0%	5.1%
2000	5.0%	−6.0%	9.9%	15.1%	−9.1%	4.1%	5.1%
1999	3.7%	2.1%	−1.9%	−8.4%	21.0%	4.7%	6.5%
1998	5.3%	1.9%	8.7%	13.7%	28.6%	4.5%	4.7%
1997	7.6%	13.0%	10.4%	11.3%	33.4%	4.5%	5.8%

Data Source: S&P Capital IQ LCD (Leveraged Loans), J.P. Morgan (High Yield Bonds, High Grade Bonds, 10-year Treasury), FactSet (S&P 500), U.S. Bureau of Economic Analysis (U.S. GDP), and U.S. Department of the Treasury (10-year treasury yield)

loans and high yield bonds against high grade debt, U.S. government debt, and the S&P 500 since 1997. Shown in Table 7.2, high yield debt produced its best returns in the years following a recession (2003 and 2009). Conversely, the asset class underperformed in the periods leading into and entering a recession. During a recession, the asset class can recover quickly as either the economy grows or shows signs of progress out of a recessionary environment. Gross domestic product (GDP) and the 10-year treasury yield are included in the table to provide a gauge of economic activity and the interest rate environment. Periods of strong GDP growth often drive asset class performance as the economic prospects of high yield issuers improve and default-related loss declines – two factors that cause the price of high yield debt to appreciate.

7.4 HIGH YIELD BOND AND LEVERAGED LOAN PRICE VOLATILITY

Historically, leveraged loans have experienced lower price volatility than high yield bonds. There are three primary reasons for this: first, leveraged loans are generally higher rated and more senior claims in the capital structure, which means they carry lower fundamental risk. Second, as discussed in Chapter 3, the loan buyer base, at the time of writing, consists of a greater proportion of investors that are committed to the asset class rather than looking at relative value more broadly. This puts leveraged loans in relatively more "stable hands" though "fast" money does at times make its way into the market, such as in 2007 and 2011, and that can subsequently lead to periods of heightened volatility. Last, bonds are securities that are more easily financed and can be sold short. When markets sell off, short selling usually intensifies pricing declines and then can lead to sharp recoveries as prices recover and short sales are covered. Leveraged loans in contrast are not securities that can be traditionally shorted.

To illustrate pricing volatility of the high yield asset class, Table 7.3 looks at the 12-month high and low price of bond and leveraged loans from 2000–2014. When looking at the data in Table 7.3, keep in mind that bond and loan prices are stated as a percentage of par. So if a loan drops from 100 to 95, it has lost 5% of its value, or provided a 5% negative return from price. Excluding 2008 and 2009, annual prices varied 9.3 points on average in the high yield bond market and 4.3 points on average in the leveraged loan market. 2008 and 2009, a period of extraordinary volatility,

TABLE 7.3　Annual High Yield Price Volatility

Leveraged Loans				High Yield Bonds			
Year	High–Low Price Δ	High	Low	Year	High–Low Price Δ	High	Low
2000	3.5	94.2	90.7	2000	13.2	86.3	73.1
2001	4.9	92.8	87.8	2001	8.6	79.2	70.6
2002	3.8	90.7	86.9	2002	9.5	78.9	69.4
2003	7.3	96.5	89.2	2003	17.7	92.8	75.1
2004	3.8	100.3	96.5	2004	9.1	101.8	92.7
2005	1.2	100.7	99.5	2005	7.0	102.9	95.9
2006	0.9	100.7	99.8	2006	4.3	99.2	94.9
2007	6.1	100.5	94.4	2007	7.9	101.0	93.1
2008	34.1	94.4	60.3	2008	37.0	93.1	56.1
2009	25.6	87.4	61.7	2009	34.4	93.4	59.0
2010	6.3	93.6	87.3	2010	9.9	102.8	92.9
2011	7.3	96.1	88.8	2011	11.3	104.1	92.8
2012	5.2	96.8	91.6	2012	5.4	104.4	99.0
2013	1.8	98.6	96.8	2013	6.7	107.0	100.3
2014	4.0	99.1	95.0	2014	10.2	105.3	95.1
Annual High–Low Price Δ 2000–2014*				**Annual High–Low Price Δ 2000–2014***			
Avg.	4.3			Avg.	9.3		
High	7.3			High	17.7		
Low	0.9			Low	4.3		

Note: Data as of December 31, 2014. *Excludes 2008 and 2009 data.
Data Source: S&P Capital IQ LCD (Leveraged Loans), J.P. Morgan (High Yield Bonds)

are excluded so not to inflate the averages. The data is significant because it shows how investment timing is more important in the bond market due to greater potential for price volatility.

When evaluating market performance, it's important to keep 2008 and 2009 in perspective. That time period represents one of the most significant periods of price volatility ever experienced in the high yield market. The extremeness of the sell-off stemmed from a confluence of factors including the recession, the heavy reliance on total return swaps and margin finance, and the failure of investment banks. The financial contagion and liquidity crisis that followed was far from ordinary. For this reason, it's often useful to look at historical data on the high yield market including and excluding performance over this time.

7.5   RETURNS BY RATINGS

Looking at the returns of high yield debt by rating provides a sense of the different opportunities available with individual debt issues within this broad asset category. The varying performance of high yield by credit rating also highlights how not all high yield exposure is the same or simply a call on the economic cycle and spreads. Table 7.4 details the annual total returns for high yield bonds and leveraged loans rated BB, B, and

TABLE 7.4   High Yield Bond and Leveraged Loan Returns by Rating

	High Yield Bonds: Total Returns			Leveraged Loans: Total Returns			10-year Treasury
Year	BB Index	B Index	CCC Index	BB Index	B Index	CCC Index	Total Return
2014	5.2%	1.5%	−2.2%	1.5%	1.4%	6.1%	10.9%
2013	4.3%	8.8%	15.3%	3.8%	5.9%	10.4%	−7.7%
2012	13.3%	15.9%	21.0%	7.2%	10.4%	18.3%	4.2%
2011	9.5%	7.7%	0.5%	2.7%	2.1%	−6.3%	17.0%
2010	13.2%	14.1%	19.7%	7.9%	11.1%	23.2%	8.3%
2009	39.0%	42.5%	112.0%	35.8%	61.2%	88.6%	−8.8%
2008	−13.2%	−28.5%	−47.1%	−24.2%	−34.9%	−45.8%	20.2%
2007	2.5%	4.4%	−0.4%	2.4%	1.1%	−1.7%	9.8%
2006	8.8%	10.4%	19.3%	6.2%	7.4%	10.7%	1.4%
2005	2.3%	3.5%	−3.1%	4.7%	5.4%	6.4%	1.9%
2004	8.8%	10.8%	18.3%	4.2%	5.6%	11.4%	4.7%
2003	17.1%	24.5%	54.3%	6.9%	12.4%	21.5%	1.7%
2002	6.1%	5.5%	−4.8%	2.6%	3.9%	−8.0%	14.6%
2001	11.1%	7.8%	−1.1%	3.5%	1.2%	−27.2%	3.7%
2000	5.6%	−6.5%	−24.7%	6.7%	3.0%	−6.2%	15.1%

Source: S&P Capital IQ LCD (Leveraged Loans), J.P. Morgan (High Yield Bonds and 10-year treasury)

CCC. The highest rated high yield debt (debt that is rated BB), tends to be more sensitive to changes in treasury yields while lower rated debt is more affected by the issuer's prospects, the economic outlook, and overall market sentiment.

7.6 BETA AND CORRELATION ANALYSIS

Beta and correlation are two concepts that are used to compare total returns and volatility across asset classes. *Beta* is calculated using a regression analysis and quantifies the volatility of a security or index in relation to another. A beta of the high yield bond market might be calculated against the S&P 500 for example. If the data produced a beta of 1, it would mean for any one 1% change in the S&P, high yield would change by 1%. Betas of greater or less than 1 therefore reflect more exaggerated or muted moves relative to the S&P 500. All else being equal, a security with higher beta is perceived to carry a higher risk than one with lower beta.

In the high yield market, the bond market has historically had a higher beta to equities than the leveraged loan market. But within each broad market segment – bonds and leveraged loans – there are a variety of individual issues with varying betas to the high yield indices. As you would expect, issues rated BB typically have a lower beta (or less than 1) compared to their relative index while CCC issues often exhibit a higher beta, making them more sensitive to market movements. Beta provides insight on how a fund, index, or issue might perform in various scenarios.

Correlation is another important term related to portfolio construction. *Correlation* measures the linear relationship between the directional moves of two data sets and ascribes a value between −1 to 1 depending on the strength of this relationship. For example, if Bond A and Bond B always move up and down together, they would have a perfect positive correlation of 1. If they moved in opposition directions, they would have a negative correlation somewhere between 0 to −1, depending on the strength of the inverse relationship. If they moved together only half the time with no meaningful connection, they would have a correlation near 0, meaning the assets are not correlated positively or negatively. Correlation analysis differs from beta analysis in that it ignores the magnitude of movements. Instead, it focuses on whether a data dependency exists that creates a more predictable directional relationship. Asset allocators building diversified portfolios often try to include some assets with a negative correlation to

TABLE 7.5 Historical Beta and Correlation

Beta 2000–2014	Leveraged Loans	High Yield Bonds	High Grade Bonds	10-year Treasury	S&P 500
Leveraged Loans	1.00	0.61	0.32	−0.33	0.21
High Yield Bonds	1.12	1.00	0.80	−0.26	0.38
Correlation 2000–2014	**Leveraged Loans**	**High Yield Bonds**	**High Grade Bonds**	**10-year Treasury**	**S&P 500**
Leveraged Loans	1.00	0.83	0.25	−0.38	0.49
High Yield Bonds	0.83	1.00	0.48	−0.22	0.64

Note: As of December 31, 2014.
Data Source: S&P Capital IQ LCD (Leveraged Loans), J.P. Morgan (High Yield Bond, High Grade Bonds,10-year Treasury), FactSet (S&P 500)

others; this way they have some assets that tend to perform when others are down.

High yield debt has historically traded with a positive correlation to equities and a negative correlation to the treasury market. This is often surprising for people to learn, as they think of high yield as an interest rate sensitive product. Being a fixed income asset class, high yield is rate sensitive, particularly the higher quality segments of the market. But representing a higher risk-return investment with performance more tied to issuer fundamentals, the asset class tends to perform well in improving economies, which can be a time when interest rates rise and treasury debt underperforms.

Table 7.5 compares the beta and correlation of the high yield bond index and loan index to other asset classes from 2000–2014. Over this time period, the high yield bond market has traded at a 0.4 beta to the S&P 500 with a 0.6 correlation. This means that directional moves are positively correlated but high yield bonds experience approximately half the volatility. At a 0.6 correlation, the strength of the relationship is not very strong and therefore shouldn't be relied upon over shorter time horizons. The correlation between high yield debt and equities improves in more extreme market moves and in sell-offs that occur over several months. The leveraged loan market has traded at a 0.6 beta to the high yield bond market and a 0.2 beta to the S&P 500. Despite difference in their payment structures, with bonds being primarily fixed rate obligations and loans being floating rate, leveraged loans have a highly positive correlation of 0.8 to high yield bonds and therefore exhibit a strong directional relationship. In relation to government debt, high yield bonds and leveraged loans are negatively correlated to 10+ year treasury debt, which means the asset class can perform as treasury yields rise.

7.7 INTEREST RATE RISK

Interest rate risk results from changes in the federal fund rates, which is the interest rate at which depository institutions lend balances held at the Federal Reserve Bank to each other overnight. The federal funds rate is set by the Federal Reserve Bank and is used as a monetary policy tool to either stimulate employment or manage the pace of inflation. Changes to this rate affect the yield curve, or treasury rate at varying maturities, because they change the outlook on interest rates. This is important because treasury debt yields serve as a benchmark for all other debt – when they increase, so must the yields of risk assets in order to maintain the same risk premium; this is why prices can decline (a price decline increases yield). Conversely, when treasury yields decline, prices of other fixed income debt can rise to reflect lower yields. As a result of risk-free rates playing such a large role in the price of all other debt, changes, and even anticipation of changes to interest rates, are closely followed by fixed income investors.

Table 7.6 examines high yield performance from 1997–2014 in rising and declining treasury yield environments. As shown, no obvious relationship exists with the high yield market as a whole: high yield has produced mostly positive returns in both periods. This data highlights how the asset class is less affected by interest rates and more by underlying credit risk and the economic environment. The fixed income market segments most sensitive to interest rate risk are those with a low risk premium and with longer-term maturities.

But this is not to say that all high yield debt is not interest rate sensitive. Different segments of the high yield market can perform relatively better or worse depending on the changes to treasury yields. Table 7.4 highlights how the performance of BB rated debt, a higher quality segment of the market, can be more closely aligned with treasury debt. It's helpful to also consider periods of rapidly rising interest rates. In these environments, leveraged loans, which have a floating rate of interest, have outperformed many asset classes including high yield bonds, investment grade bonds, and treasury debt. Table 7.7 summarizes the four periods over the past 15 years where the Federal Reserve Bank increased the

TABLE 7.6 Impact of Interest Rates on High Yield Debt

Year	US Treasury Yields		Asset Class Indices – Total Return			
	10 Year	10-year Change	10-year Treasury	High Grade Bonds	High Yield Bonds	Leveraged Loans
Rising Yields						
2013	3.04%	1.26%	−7.7%	−0.8%	8.2%	5.3%
2009	3.85%	1.60%	−8.8%	18.5%	58.2%	51.6%
2006	4.71%	0.32%	1.4%	3.8%	11.6%	6.8%
2005	4.39%	0.15%	1.9%	1.4%	2.4%	5.1%
2003	4.27%	0.44%	1.7%	8.2%	26.8%	10.0%
1999	6.45%	1.80%	−8.4%	−1.9%	2.1%	3.7%
Declining Yields						
2014	2.17%	−0.87%	10.9%	7.8%	2.2%	1.6%
2012	1.78%	−0.11%	4.2%	9.9%	15.4%	9.7%
2011	1.89%	−1.41%	17.0%	8.7%	7.0%	1.5%
2010	3.30%	−0.55%	8.3%	9.3%	14.7%	10.1%
2008	2.25%	−1.79%	20.2%	0.5%	−26.6%	−29.1%
2007	4.04%	−0.67%	9.8%	6.0%	2.6%	2.0%
2004	4.24%	−0.03%	4.7%	6.0%	11.1%	5.2%
2002	3.83%	−1.24%	14.6%	10.7%	3.2%	1.9%
2001	5.07%	−0.05%	3.7%	10.7%	6.7%	4.2%
2000	5.12%	−1.33%	15.1%	9.9%	−6.0%	5.0%
1998	4.65%	−1.10%	13.7%	8.7%	1.9%	5.3%
1997	5.75%	−0.68%	11.3%	10.4%	13.0%	7.6%

Data Source: S&P Capital IQ LCD (Leveraged Loans), J.P. Morgan (High Yield Bonds, High Grade Bonds, 10-year Treasury), FactSet (S&P 500), and U.S. Department of the Treasury (10-year treasury yield)

federal funds target rate four times or more over a 12-month time period. During this 48-month time period, leveraged loans produced consistently attractive risk-adjusted returns with only three negative total return months versus 15 for high yield bonds, 16 for the S&P 500, 19 for high grade bonds, and 22 for the 10-year treasury index. With a 7.3 Sharpe ratio over these time periods, this data supports the case for investing in leveraged loans during periods of economic growth and more rapidly rising interest rates.

TABLE 7.7   High Yield Performance When Interest Rates Rise More Rapidly

	Avg. Return	Avg. Vol.	Avg. Sharpe	Total # of Neg. Months
Leveraged Loans	5.3%	1.0%	7.3	3
High Yield Bonds	5.3%	3.3%	2.0	15
S&P 500	10.5%	9.4%	1.4	16
High Grade Bonds	2.8%	3.7%	0.7	19
10-year Treasury	2.1%	5.7%	0.3	22

Note: The above analysis reflects the 4, 12 month time periods since 1999 that the Federal Reserve has increased the federal funds target rate 4 times or more (June 1999 – May 2000, 2004, 2005, 2006).
Data Source: S&P Capital IQ LCD (Leveraged Loans), J.P. Morgan (High Yield Bonds, High Grade Bonds, 10-year Treasury), FactSet (S&P 500)

When considering the performance of leveraged loans, it must be noted that due to the zero interest rate policy (ZIRP) implemented by the Federal Reserve in 2008, high yield market-makers established LIBOR floors to provide a minimum rate for LIBOR. As discussed in previous chapters, leveraged loans are usually priced on a spread to LIBOR, which is considered a risk-free rate that moves in tandem with other risk-free rates such as the federal funds rate. At year-end 2014, the majority of leveraged loans outstanding had a LIBOR floor set at approximately 100 bps on average.[1] This is important to keep in mind because interest payments on leveraged loans will not increase until the LIBOR rate exceeds a loan's LIBOR floor.

7.8   DEFAULTS AND RECOVERIES

High yield default rates vary for bonds and loans and so do recovery rates. *Recovery rates*, or *recoveries,* represent the principal value remaining post default. Over time, bonds have posted an average default rate of 3.8% with a 41% recovery.[2] This means that on average 3.8% of the high yield

---

[1] S&P Capital IQ LCD.
[2] Moody's Investors Service and J.P. Morgan – "J.P. Morgan High Yield Default Monitor – December 2014."

bond universe experiences a default in a year, which causes a 59% loss of principal. Leveraged loans have posted a slightly lower average default rate of 3.5% and have a higher average recovery of 69%.[3] Recoveries ultimately matter more than default rates because they relate directly to the level of principal impairment or loss – a source of negative return. As one would expect, higher rated debt has higher recoveries than lower rated debt. Recoveries by rating also tend to be comparable for both bonds and loans. The reason the bond index posts lower recoveries than the loan index is because it contains a proportionately higher amount of lower rated and unsecured debt.

During recessions, high yield debt tends to experience a spike in default rates as well as a drop in recoveries. The reason for this is not just the fact that highly indebted issuers are sensitive to economic growth, its also the result of a loosening of lending standards during the preceding period of economic expansion, which, in turn leads to weaker protection for creditors. For example, excessive confidence prior to the 2001 recession allowed many low quality telecom related companies access to the high yield market. The 2008 recession was preceded by an exceedingly large number of highly leveraged, large-cap leveraged buyouts that had complex capital structures and lower margin of safety for junior creditors. These types of companies experienced above average default rates and had debt that experienced lower recoveries when economic conditions changed.

Table 7.8 shows the historical default rate experience of high yield bonds and leveraged loans from 1998 to 2014. Default rates and recoveries are included and the 17-year average for high yield bonds and leveraged loans are shown to provide a long-term average for comparison. This long-term average is often used to calculate the normalized default-loss premium of high yield credit spreads, a topic addressed in Chapter 8.

7.9　SUMMARY

The performance of high yield explains why the asset class has grown 10-fold in size since the early 1990s and prospered into a $2.5 trillion industry. Over the past two decades, bond and leveraged loans have produced attractive risk-adjusted returns compared to other U.S. asset classes

---

[3]Moody's Investors Service and J.P. Morgan - "J.P. Morgan High Yield Default Monitor – December 2014."

TABLE 7.8   Historical Default Rate Experience

High Yield Universe			Leveraged Loan Universe		
Year	Default Rate	All High Yield Recovery	Year	Default Rate	First Lien Recovery
1998	1.7%	38.3%	1998	1.5%	56.7%
1999	4.1%	33.8%	1999	4.2%	73.5%
2000	5.0%	25.3%	2000	6.6%	68.8%
2001	9.1%	21.8%	2001	6.3%	64.9%
2002	8.0%	29.7%	2002	6.0%	58.8%
2003	3.3%	40.4%	2003	2.3%	73.4%
2004	1.1%	58.5%	2004	1.0%	87.7%
2005	2.8%	56.0%	2005	3.0%	83.8%
2006	0.9%	55.0%	2006	0.5%	83.6%
2007	0.4%	54.7%	2007	0.2%	68.6%
2008	2.3%	26.9%	2008	3.7%	58.1%
2009	10.3%	35.7%	2009	12.8%	61.4%
2010	0.8%	41.0%	2010	1.8%	71.2%
2011	1.7%	48.6%	2011	0.4%	67.0%
2012	1.3%	53.2%	2012	1.4%	55.3%
2013	0.7%	52.7%	2013	1.7%	68.6%
2014	1.6%	51.2%	2014	1.7%	71.6%
Long-term Average	3.8%	41.3%	Long-term Average	3.5%	68.8%

Note: As of December 31, 2014. Shaded years represent recessionary time periods. 2014 default rates exclude TXU Corp.'s $36.1 billion default.
Data Source: J.P. Morgan, Markit

including equities, investment grade debt, and treasuries making them an important component of many diversified portfolios and particularly those seeking current income. While bonds and loans have exhibited a positive correlation over most time periods, bonds have historically had a higher beta to equities than loans and are more price volatile. Correlations between bonds and loans, as well as those between different segments of the high yield market such as high and low rated debt, can break down as the economic cycle evolves and the prospects of rate changes increase. During periods of recession, both bonds and leveraged loans can experience higher defaults and lower recoveries as excesses from the boom years are worked off. During periods of economic growth and rising rates, leveraged loans can outperform bonds through greater price stability and interest rate protection. An understanding of why and how high yield debt performance varies provides a framework for assessing the different investment strategies and fund types that provide high yield exposure.

CHAPTER 8

Assessing the Market Opportunity

A ssessing the high yield market opportunity requires gathering information on the market, formulating a view on credit spreads, and assessing the market outlook. As an over-the-counter market with many private issuers that don't report financials publicly, high yield can lack transparency and be difficult to track. But ranging from investment banks to third-party firms to rating agencies, there are various places to look for insight and data on the high yield market. High yield value can be assessed by breaking down its risk premium into simpler components and then comparing these inputs to historical experience to formulate a view on the market outlook. Any prospective view of high yield performance also involves tracking issuer fundamentals and technical considerations such as supply and demand trends. Chapter 8 provides insight on how market participants can track and assess the high yield market.

8.1 SOURCES OF MARKET INFORMATION

Intelligence on the high yield market can be gathered from several groups including investment banks, third-party news and research firms, rating agencies, industry bodies, and the government. The largest investment banks devote many resources to support the market's functioning. This includes employing large research teams that produce in-depth research on market trends on a daily basis. Industry growth has also created a role for third-party information providers. These firms provide everything from news coverage to historical databases to credit agreement assessments. Also, rating agencies, industry groups, and the government collect and report data related to high yield risk and activity.

Investment banks: There are over a dozen investment banks that publish research on the high yield market. Some of the publications are standard and come out daily, reporting on spreads, prices, and total returns. Others are more bespoke and provide relative value comparisons, in-depth historical studies, and investment recommendations. Of course, part of their interest in doing this is to support business that might be derived from other areas of the bank such as trading and investment banking, but much of the analysis provided is objective and provided for the benefit of interested market participants. A relationship with the investment bank or subscription is generally required for access to their high yield research.

Third-party news and research firms: Third-party research is distinguished from investment banks by having no conflicts of interest that could result from the underwriting or trading of high yield debt. News providers publish information for an audience that includes fund managers, private equity investors, corporate lawyers, investment bankers, and others. The most well-known news providers include S&P Capital IQ Leveraged Commentary and Data Group (S&P LCD), Debtwire, Thomson Reuters LPC, and Bloomberg. These firms provide real-time news coverage on the high yield market that most market participants consider important. S&P LCD, for example, not only provides exceptional news coverage but also produces weekly, monthly, and quarterly reports with detailed trends. Bloomberg produces news coverage and also provides terminals that are used by dealers and market participants to communicate information and trade high yield debt.

MarketAxess, Markit, and IDC provide secondary price levels of individual bonds and loans and information on market depth or the number of dealers trading a particular issue. Pricing services are important for investors, valuation firms, and financing providers because they provide quotes from which portfolios can be *marked-to-market* or valued at market prices to establish collateral and net asset values. Yield Book provides index data and portfolio management tools derived from its extensive database.

Lipper FMI and EPFR distribute information related to capital flows into high yield retail funds. Fund flows are used by market participants to gauge technical trends and retail investor sentiment. Covenant Review provides legal assessments of credit agreements of high yield issues. By breaking down complex documents into more simplified summaries, Covenant Review helps investors better understand the structural protections and deficiencies of individual debt instruments.

Rating agencies, industry bodies, and the government: Information on the high yield market can also be obtained from groups more involved with its functioning. The Loan Syndications and Trading Association (LSTA) is an industry group that promotes corporate loans and provides market data as well as an index, the S&P/LSTA Leveraged Loan Index. Through its TRACE platform, the Financial Industry Regulatory Authority (FINRA) provides information on the secondary trading volume of certain high yield securities. While FINRA used to only track registered bonds, it now also tracks 144A bonds, which allows FINRA TRACE to provide a more complete picture of the high yield bond market's trading volume. Several years ago, the Federal Reserve Bank of New York began publishing the net holdings of high yield corporate bonds of the 22 primary banks and securities broker-dealers that serve as trading counterparties of the New York Fed. This provides insight on whether investment banks are expanding or shrinking their balance sheets of corporate debt, which can add supply or create demand. Last, the three major rating agencies meet with individual issuers and assign credit ratings to their debt. In addition to issuing ratings, rating agencies publish and provide data on market trends including spreads, default rates, and recoveries.

8.2 HOW TO EVALUATE HIGH YIELD CREDIT SPREADS

Understanding how to evaluate high yield credit spreads is important to assessing the value of high yield debt. Discussed in Chapter 4, credit spreads can be deconstructed into a risk-free rate and a risk premium. The risk-free rate is typically three-month LIBOR for leveraged loans and the five-year treasury yield for high yield bonds; it is the benchmark yield for fixed income investments. Any risk asset must at least pay this amount to compensate for the possibility of default loss. The additional compensation that attracts investors is known as the risk premium. Evaluating credit spreads involves forming a view on whether the risk premium over, under, or fairly compensates for the risk.

When it comes to evaluating the spreads of individual debt issues, investors conduct due diligence on the company to gain a sense of risk return versus comparable opportunities available in the market. When it comes to valuing the market, issuer-specific risks become marginalized by market diversity. Factors that affect market performance include interest rates, the economy, U.S. currency, commodity prices, and fundamental market trends such as interest coverage and leverage ratios. Unfortunately, there is no model that can accurately incorporate all these factors, which are constantly changing. High yield research analysts do build sophisticated multi-variable models that produce estimates of fair value. These can be helpful but can also seem like black-box forecasting, as it's sometimes unclear how all the inputs come together to derive estimates.

In my experience, I've found it helpful to estimate fair value spreads based on a simple formula and then compare this value to index spreads. A basic method to estimate credit spreads focuses on three variables: (1) defaults, (2) default loss severity, and (3) excess spread or illiquidity premium. The values for this equation can be obtained from different sources. Default loss expectations can be estimated from historical experience or long-term averages. Rating agencies as well as high yield research analysts also provide forward-looking default rate estimates for both the high yield bond and leveraged loan markets. Default loss severity relates to what amount of loss occurs in default scenarios. The bond market has historically experienced a 59% principal loss from defaults while leveraged loans have resulted in a 32% principal loss.[1] These values can be used as part of this equation. Or, if recent experience suggests recoveries might be lower than long-term, average experience would tend to suggest, more conservative estimates can be used. In Chapter 7, we list historical default rates and recoveries so that periods of market stress can be scrutinized and a broader range of historical outcomes is known.

Of all the metrics that drive credit spreads, excess spread is the most difficult to quantify. Excess spread can be thought of as the premium

---

[1]Moody's Investors Service; J.P. Morgan "J.P. Morgan Default Monitor, June 2015."

provided to compensate for the risk that a high yield bond or loan is less liquid or less easily sold. Quantifying the value of liquidity is imperfect in part because buyers have different liquidity needs and the buyer base fluctuates constantly. Mutual funds and ETFs for example must provide their investors with daily liquidity, which makes liquidity critical to them. Private investment funds care less about daily liquidity and more about long-term value. Approximately 50% of the high yield bond market consists of issues that are less than $500 million in size.[2] While these are often syndicated to large groups of investors, they do not maintain the same liquidity as larger markets like those in government treasuries. In stressed environments, this can become an important consideration as the illiquidity premium can cause smaller issues to underperform. In 2008, for example, when the market became one-sided with sellers, illiquidity premium shot up significantly creating spreads far in excess of what expected defaults and recoveries might imply.

Historical excess spread can be calculated by subtracting historical default loss experience from actual spreads. Using this approach, excess spreads have averaged 372 bps for leveraged loans since 1997 and 358 bps for high yield bonds since 2000.[3] The higher excess spread for loans accounts for that market having less liquidity or annual turnover than bonds. These values can serve as a good proxy for estimating the fair value of spreads in environments where the high yield market is properly functioning and not experiencing strain or risk aversion.

Table 8.1 puts these components together to calculate a fair value for loan and bond spreads as of June 2015. As shown, using estimated default rates, expected loss and historical excess spread, the fair value of the leveraged loan and high yield bond indices was 435 bps and 534 bps, respectively.

Shown in Table 8.1, the actual spreads of high yield bond and leveraged loans as of June 30, 2015 were higher than fair value estimates. This suggests that either (1) spreads overly compensated for risks and presented value or (2) the market was pricing in higher default risk and/or illiquidity premium. The expected default rate would have to increase to 4.9% for leveraged loans and 3.3% for high yield bonds for the index spreads to be justified by the default rate outlook. Spreads priced loans at a higher default rate than bonds, despite it being the less risky asset class historically. The analysis could therefore conclude that loan spreads offered attractive

---

[2]BofA Merrill Lynch Global Research.
[3]S&P Capital IQ LCD, J.P. Morgan.

TABLE 8.1 Credit Spread Analysis

	Leveraged Loans	High Yield Bonds
Est. Default Rate in 12 Months (bps)	200	300
x Expected Loss (bps)	32	59
Credit Loss Premium (bps)	63	176
Long Term Avg. Excess Spread (bps)	372	358
+ Credit Loss Premium (bps)	63	176
Fair Value Spread (bps)	435	534
As of 6/30/2015		
Current Credit Spread (bps)	526	549
Room for Compression based on Fair Value (bps)	91	16

Note: As of June 30, 2015.
Source: S&P Capital IQ LCD (Leveraged Loans), J.P. Morgan (High Yield Bonds)

absolute value compared to fair value estimates and more relative value than bonds. The bond market in comparison appeared more fairly priced.

8.3 PUTTING HISTORICAL CREDIT SPREADS INTO CONTEXT

The next step to evaluating credit spreads is to put them in historical context. This provides a sense of value relative to historical periods and can also provide a context of upside and downside potential. Table 8.2 shows historical credit spreads for high yield bonds and leveraged loans from 2003 through June 2015. Spreads can vary based on the economic environment, market conditions, and investor sentiment toward the asset class, any of which can change unexpectedly. When the economy and stock market were growing in the mid-2000s period, default loss and illiquidity premium declined and spreads compressed. Loan and bond spreads compressed to lows of 222 bps and 266 bps, respectively. In the depths of the Great Recession, these spreads soared to 2,474 bps and 1,929 bps. A forward-looking estimate for credit spreads, which can be

TABLE 8.2 Historical High Yield Loan and Bond Spreads

Leveraged Loan Index			High Yield Bond Index		
	Spread	**Price**		**Spread**	**Price**
Today	**526**	**97.8**	**Today**	**549**	**96.7**
Year	**Avg. Spread**	**Avg. Price**	**Year**	**Avg. Spread**	**Avg. Price**
2015	520	98.0	2015	542	98.2
2014	479	98.8	2014	454	102.9
2013	505	98.5	2013	491	103.7
2012	613	95.8	2012	625	102.0
2011	606	95.0	2011	624	100.8
2010	611	93.3	2010	659	97.9
2009	1294	79.5	2009	1100	76.7
2008	1481	76.5	2008	962	82.3
2007	323	98.0	2007	385	97.8
2006	240	100.3	2006	355	97.0
2005	242	100.6	2005	380	99.1
2004	293	100.3	2004	442	96.7
2003	450	97.0	2003	679	85.4

Note: As of June 30, 2015.
Source: S&P Capital IQ LCD (Leveraged Loan Index), J.P. Morgan (High Yield Bond Index)

derived from research analyst reports or the spread model provided, is helpful, but this value should also be put in historical context to gain a sense of value and volatility potential.

Please keep in mind that the fair value model I outlined above is an imperfect proxy. Even comparisons to historical spreads are not entirely appropriate due to changes that occur in the index, such as with the weighted average ratings or duration of constituents. But as a practitioner, fair value estimates and comparisons to historical periods can be helpful in providing some basis for contextualizing value.

8.4 TRACKING ISSUER FUNDAMENTALS

Tracking trends in issuer fundamentals provides insight on how high yield credit quality is changing and enables a determination of whether market risks are developing. In the equity markets, it's possible to gain a clear

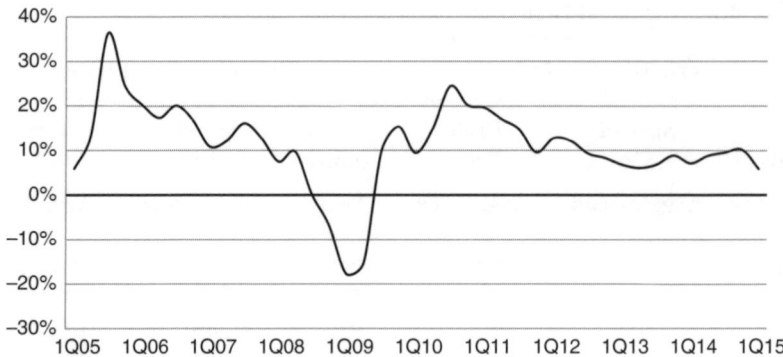

FIGURE 8.1   Quarterly EBITDA Growth
Source: S&P Capital IQ LCD

perspective at the end of earnings season on how S&P 500 or Dow Jones Industrial Average constituents performed on revenue and earnings versus prior year or Wall Street estimates. Unfortunately, the high yield market does not have this level of transparency. The leveraged loan and high yield bond market consists of approximately 25% and 50% publicly reporting issuers, respectively.[4] Quarterly data from these issuers offers a partial picture of revenue and EBITDA growth in the market along with trends in leverage and interest coverage ratios. Figure 8.1 shows quarterly year-over-year EBITDA growth for high yield issuers that publicly file. As with other trend analyses, accelerating or decelerating trends are important to track because they signal in which direction fundamental trends are heading.

In order to gain a more complete understanding of issuer fundamentals, real insight can be gained from assessing trends in the primary market, where information on new issues is disseminated more broadly. The types of newly issued debt along with leverage levels and interest coverage ratios can provide a sense of the fundamental risk in the market. When unproven businesses or business models gain access to the market, like some technology and telecom companies did in the early 2000s, it lays the foundation for the next major market correction. Similarly, when risk tolerance increases and more marginal debt issues can be raised, such as holding company notes from the 2005–2007 time period, default losses eventually spike.

Two important metrics related to fundamental risk that can be tracked through new issues are the LBO leverage and interest coverage ratios.

---

[4]S&P Capital IQ LCD and BofA Merrill Lynch Global Research.

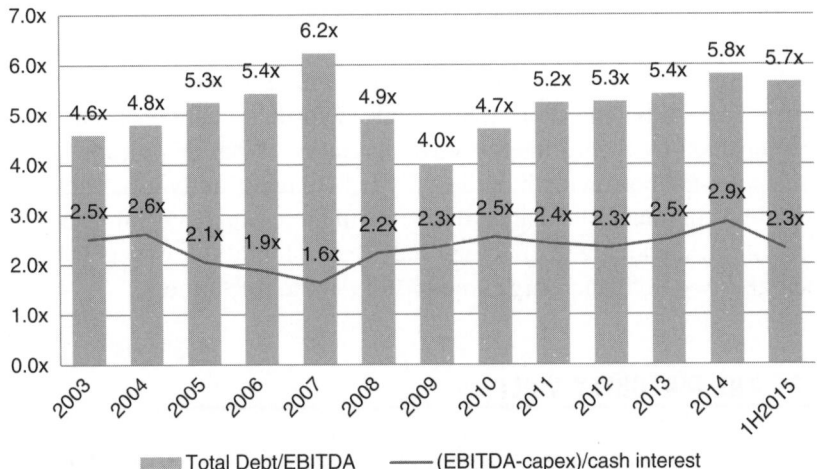

FIGURE 8.2   Large Corp. LBO Leverage and Cash Interest Coverage
Source: S&P Capital IQ LCD

LBO leverage reflects the total amount of debt issued in connection with leveraged buyouts and is stated as a multiple to EBITDA. All else being equal the higher the ratio, the greater the risks. Interest coverage ratios speak less to the quantum of debt and more to the issuer's ability to make interest payments. The interest coverage ratio is calculated by dividing the amount of annual interest expense by EBITDA. Companies with a higher interest coverage ratio have greater ability to withstand adversity and stay current on interest payments.

The reason these metrics are important to follow is because defaults and corporate bankruptcies are usually triggered by an issuer's inability to make interest or principal payments. This inability can be driven by debt maturities, insufficient liquidity, and a declining creditworthiness of issuers. Shown in Figure 8.2, historical LBO leverage and interest coverage ratios clearly point to the risks that were developing in 2007. At the time, LBO leverage levels reached a peak at 6.2x EBITDA and interest coverage ratios reached a low of 1.6x. This meant higher risk with less downside flexibility. The preceding period of low defaults and positive returns had led the market to lend on increasingly aggressive terms. Fundamentals deteriorated significantly over the period from 2003 through 2007 and, as this occurred, credit spreads compressed too (data available in Table 8.2). The losses that occurred in 2008 and 2009 were amplified by the excessive risk-taking that had occurred in the preceding five years.

In the period following the Great Recession from 2009–2014, leverage multiples have increased from recessionary lows and are now approaching 2007 levels. While this is a trend that warrants caution – particularly as it relates to buying more junior high yield debt claims – it has been accompanied by record interest coverage ratios. What this means is that companies are borrowing more heavily but at significantly lower costs. If this trend continues, the market outlook will increasingly be influenced by interest rates, which will affect not only the cash flows of issuers but also their ability to refinance large amounts of debt in the future.

8.5 THE MATURITY WALL

Coming out of the Great Recession, the high yield market was facing a large *maturity wall,* a term that refers to a point in the near future where a substantial amount of high yield debt becomes due. In 2009, there was concern that issuers might struggle to refinance this debt, particularly if the economy took a turn for the worse and/or capital markets became more difficult to access, and this would lead to a more severe default cycle. Favorable market conditions ultimately allowed high yield issuers to refinance most of this debt, and today the high yield market has no significant upcoming maturities in the next few years.

Figure 8.3 shows high yield debt maturities through 2023. The bulk of high yield maturities now fall in the 2019–2021 time period. While the maturity wall is an important metric to follow, it's important to keep in mind that debt maturities are not necessarily a leading indicator of defaults. Defaults are driven more by issuer fundamentals and the state of the economy. Fewer near term debt maturities is better for the market outlook though; it implies that existing issuers are less reliant on capital markets access. But the pushing out of a maturity wall should not be overly relied upon as an assurance for a continuing low default environment.

8.6 MONITORING EXCESSIVE RISK-TAKING

Excessive risk-taking occurs when increased confidence and investor demand create more marginal supply of high yield debt. One way marginal supply can be tracked is by the growth in lower rated debt issued, which is shown in Figure 8.4. In 2008 for instance, driven by strong demand

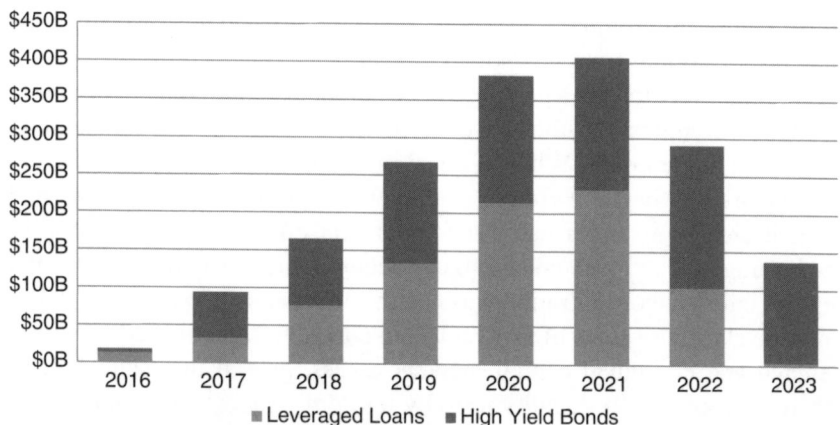

FIGURE 8.3 High Yield Market Maturity Wall
Note: As of August 14th, 2015.
Source: S&P Capital IQ LCD, J.P. Morgan

and confidence, issuance in loans and bonds rated B/CCC reached a high, amounting to 41% of all high yield issuance. Similar to the problematic growth in sub-prime lending during that same period, there was visible evidence of a problem in credit quality developing. Tracking the growth in

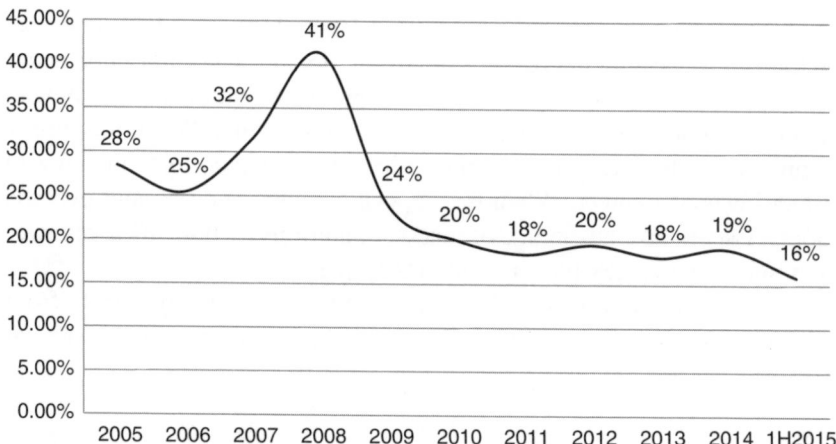

FIGURE 8.4 Lower Rated Debt Issuance for High Yield Bonds and Leveraged Loans – B/CCC or Lower
Source: S&P Capital IQ LCD

lower rated debt provides a means to monitor this trend and problems that may be developing from less sound issuance.

Another way to gain a perspective on potential defaults is by examining the types of industries that account for new issuance and outstanding secondary market debt. When cyclical industries more easily gain access to the market or begin to compose a larger share of outstanding high yield debt, it creates a clearer catalyst for defaults. In 2001, roughly 16% of the leveraged loan index consisted of telecom issuers, whereas the second highest industry concentration was health care at approximately 8%.[5] The unfunded business plans of many telecom companies, predicated on strong demand and continued capital markets access, proved unsustainable. In 2001, eight of the 36 defaults were by telecom issuers.[6] Telecom issuers significantly affected the default rate, which remained between 5.50%–7.25% from June 2001 through April 2003, nearly twice the historical average.[7] As of June 2015, the largest industry in the high yield market is energy, which accounts for roughly 16% of the bond market and 5% of the leveraged loan market.[8] The decline in oil prices starting in the second half of 2014 and continuing through the first half of 2015 has caused an increase in the default rates, led by the energy sector.

8.7 HIGH YIELD SUPPLY AND DEMAND

Market technicals – such as the supply and demand for high yield debt – can be tracked to varying degrees for bonds and loans. Assessing imbalances can provide insight on why actual credit spreads might deviate from what issuer fundamentals and other market indicators signal. When the supply of high yield debt exceeds demand, prices decline and yields increase to attract investor interest. When the opposite occurs, and demand exceeds supply, issuers take advantage of market conditions by borrowing at lower rates and on more flexible terms in higher quantities.

Of the two, supply is easier to track because it mostly results from new debt issues, which are publicly marketed and can be tracked from the

---

[5]S&P Capital IQ LCD (S&P/ LSTA Leveraged Loan Index).
[6]Ibid.
[7]Ibid.
[8]BofA Merrill Lynch Global Research (BofA Merrill Lynch US High Yield Master II Index) and S&P Capital IQ LCD (S&P LSTA Leveraged Loan Index).

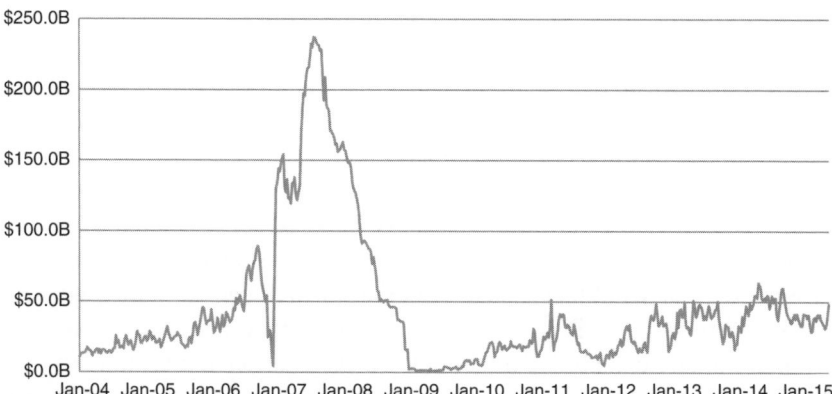

FIGURE 8.5 Institutional Loan Forward Calendar
Source: S&P Capital IQ LCD

new issue forward calendar and completed transactions that trade into the secondary market. The new issue forward calendar is compiled by several sources including S&P Capital IQ Leveraged Commentary and Data and lists all high yield new issues in the market or expected to be sold. Figure 8.5 shows a weekly analysis of the forward calendar for institutional leveraged loans back to 2004. When new issue supply is large, as it was in 2007, the market is more vulnerable to a correction as investors will often sell a portion of their current holdings to make room for new investments, in turn putting pricing pressure on the secondary market.

When assessing supply it's helpful to look at net supply or the amount of incremental debt being raised, as many high yield transactions relate to refinancing existing debt – transactions that do not always require much new demand. While there are other components that affect net supply including interest payments, amortization and repayments, these are less easy to track and are secondary considerations to the amount of new debt being raised.

Demand for high yield debt is more tricky to assess and can be better tracked for leveraged loans than for high yield bonds. High yield debt is held by a broad group of investors, most of whom do not disclose their holdings. As a result, only demand from retail funds such as mutual funds, ETFs, and closed-end funds can be tracked. These funds publicly report their holdings and assets under management. Lipper FMI and EPFR provide data from over 300 high yield bonds and leveraged loans that aggregates capital inflows and outflows to retail funds. It's important to keep in mind that retail funds represent less than 25% of the high yield bond market and the data therefore does not provide a complete picture of demand. But since high yield retail funds are highly active market participants, their impact on marginal demand can be significant and retail fund flows has become a metric closely followed by market participants.

With approximately 60%–70% of leveraged loan new issues bought by CLOs and retail leveraged loan funds, demand for leveraged loans can be better tracked than demand for high yield bonds. Wells Fargo and J.P. Morgan regularly publish robust CLO data, which can be combined with Lipper FMI and EPFR retail fund data to provide a clearer picture of leveraged loan demand. By tracking CLO origination and fund flows into retail funds, an understanding of how much new issue volume the loan market can absorb before pricing, spreads, and yield are affected can be developed. This data doesn't necessarily have to be compiled; high yield research analysts publish information that can be used to formulate a view on the technical outlook.

8.8 SUMMARY

As an over-the-counter traded market with limited publicly available information, tracking the high yield market can be difficult and requires information from several disparate sources. Over time, news coverage, data services, and Wall Street research on high yield have significantly improved. This has provided more resources for market participants to understand the state of the market, whether credits spreads offer value, and how credit quality is trending. While there are many metrics that can be used to assess the high yield market, focusing on credit spreads, default probability, issuer fundamentals, and the market technicals that can be tracked can provide a good perspective on the market opportunity. Data on supply and demand, while imperfect, can provide a sense of whether imbalances exists that might alter short-term positioning. For longer term investors, credit fundamentals and excess spread matter most.

CHAPTER 9

1940 Act High Yield Investment Funds

The Investment Company Act of 1940, more commonly referred to as the 1940 Act, is the primary source of regulation for mutual funds and closed-end funds. In the high yield market, there are various types of 1940 Act funds available for both institutional investors and "retail" investors, or individuals who buy in smaller quantities for their personal account. These include high yield mutual funds, closed-end funds, exchange traded funds (ETFs), and business development companies. All 1940 Act funds act similarly in that they pool capital to build portfolios with diversity that individual investors would have difficulty replicating. With the bar for investing in individual high yield debt issues set high, many market participants find it sensible to gain high yield market exposure through 1940 Act funds. Today, there are over 300 such funds providing U.S. high yield exposure to choose from. This chapter provides an overview of the different 1940 Act fund structures and the pros and cons of each as it relates to gaining high yield bond and leveraged loan exposure.

9.1 THE INVESTMENT COMPANY ACT OF 1940

The Investment Company Act of 1940, also known as the 1940 Act, was enacted by Congress in 1940 following the aftermath of the 1929 stock market crash to provide more financial regulation of investment funds. Any investment manager that manages a 1940 Act fund such as Fidelity, BlackRock, Vanguard, or PIMCO, must adhere to the rules of the 1940 Act.

For investors, the 1940 Act provides important statutory protections that are enforced by the SEC. In exchange for adhering to these protections, fund managers can raise large sums of capital from the public and also create funds that operate as tax-efficient, pass-through organizations, provided certain requirements are met.

While the operating mechanics and fees of closed-end funds, mutual funds, and ETFs differ, they must all abide by certain 1940 Act rules. These include a limitation on the use of fund leverage and a tax requirement to distribute substantially all earnings. Other than business development companies, most 1940 Act funds cannot have more than 50% of net assets or one-third of the total portfolio funded with borrowings. They must also distribute at least 90% of income and capital gains in order to be treated as a regulated investment company (RIC) under the Internal Revenue Code of 1986. These two provisions alone provide some limit on the amount of risk-taking that can occur through leverage and ensure distributable income is paid out. Other rules that all 1940 Act funds must abide by relate to governance and periodic net asset value reporting. These provisions are intended to ensure that the fund adheres to its mandate and provides investors with transparency on its financial health.

1940 Act funds can elect to be open-end, closed-end, or a unit investment trust. Open-end funds must provide investors with the ability to redeem their capital on a daily basis and therefore must maintain ample liquidity. Closed-end funds and unit investment trusts do not have this requirement and instead trade in the secondary market at a discount or premium to *net asset value (NAV)*, which is calculated by taking the market value of all assets less liabilities and then dividing this amount by the number of issued shares. Investment funds can also choose to be diversified or non-diversified. Diversified funds cannot have more than 5% of their assets in any one issuer and 25% in any one industry, unless they receive an exemption. Another major distinction funds make is whether to employ an active or passive investment strategy. Active strategies use credit selection and sometimes leverage and seek to outperform an index. Passive strategies, such as those made popular by Vanguard, have low fees and seek to replicate index returns.

9.2 HIGH YIELD MUTUAL FUNDS

Mutual funds are the most popular means for retail investors to gain high yield exposure. At year-end 2014, there were approximately 375 high yield mutual funds which had over $450 billion of assets under management.[1] Most high yield mutual funds operate as open-end funds that do not use leverage. Investors in open-end mutual funds buy shares from the fund itself rather than purchase shares from other investors on a secondary market such as the New York Stock Exchange or NASDAQ Stock Market. When investors want to sell their shares, they sell them back to the fund at the current NAV per share less any applicable fees such as *deferred sales loads* or redemption fees.

The benefit of open-end mutual funds is that they provide daily liquidity to investors at the NAV. However, in order to do this, open-end funds must maintain sufficient liquidity, which means not all cash can be deployed into income-yielding assets. Taxes are another consideration when investing in open-end mutual funds. When redemptions occur, the fund can choose to use its cash or sell assets, which is a realization event that may produce more taxes depending on the type of capital gain. The main disadvantage of open-end mutual funds relative to closed-end funds and ETFs are the various fees and expenses charged that negatively impact returns. These include sales loads, redemption fees, management fees, expenses, and 12b-1 fees. To complicate matters, mutual funds offer different share classes of the same fund, which carry different fee structures. Before investing, it is always best to contact the fund directly to understand what fees and minimum initial investments are associated with different share classes.

Table 9.1 lists the top five open-end high yield bond mutual funds by assets under management (AUM) in 2014 and compares their performance against the JPM US High Yield index. When looking at performance, it is important to keep in mind that returns are stated without sales load and other fees that can vary based on investment size or for institutional and individual investors. Though many of the funds below have performance that comes close to the index, the sales load fees for some funds are quite significant in comparison to the annual returns. This makes open-end mutual funds more punitive to smaller investors that have to pay higher sales loads, and especially for those investors that have a short investment horizon and do not amortize this entry or exit cost over a longer period. Within the funds listed in Table 9.1, it is worth noting that Vanguard operates with a low-cost expense structure and no sales load. BlackRock's performance has been impressive particularly given the size of the fund. The Fidelity fund produced excellent results in 2014, but this was partially

---

[1]Lipper FMI.

TABLE 9.1 Performance of Largest High Yield Bond Mutual Funds

| Top 5 Funds | AUM ($B) | Annualized Total Returns as of 12/31/2014 | | | Fees | |
		1-Yr	3-Yr	5-Yr	Total Operating Expenses	Initial / Deferred
Benchmark: JPM US High Yield Index	$788.9	2.2%	8.5%	9.4%	–	–
American Funds High-Income Trust	$18.9	0.5%	7.0%	7.5%	0.7%	3.8%
Vanguard High-Yield Corporate Inv	$16.8	4.6%	7.7%	8.5%	0.2%	0.0%
BlackRock High Yield Bond Portfolio	$14.9	3.0%	9.4%	9.7%	0.9%	4.0%
PIMCO High Yield Fund	$10.4	3.0%	7.4%	7.9%	0.9%	3.8%
Fidelity Capital & Income	$10.4	6.1%	10.7%	9.3%	0.7%	0.0%*

Note: As of December 31, 2014. *Sales fees of 1.0% only apply within a 0–90 redemption period.
Source: Morningstar, J.P. Morgan

due to the fact that the fund has a dual mandate with a portion of its holdings in stocks including those of Alibaba at the time. Understanding the source of outperformance is often helpful to gaining a sense of its repeatability.

Open-end bank loan mutual funds are the most popular means of gaining leveraged loan exposure today. The largest leveraged loan or what is commonly called "bank loan" mutual funds generally employ active investment strategies and do not use fund leverage. Compared to the index and without sales load fees, these funds in general have performed well over time. The investment considerations for bank loan funds are similar to bond funds and relate to understanding the fee structure, source of performance, and an assessment of sustainability.

With open-end bank loan funds, including ETFs, investors must also give fund liquidity good consideration. Unlike bond transactions, which settle at T+3, or three days after the trade date, standard settlement for leveraged loans is T+7 or longer. As a result, open-end loan mutual funds operate with a mismatch in the timing in which they must meet redemptions versus receiving proceeds from asset sales. To address this, loan fund

TABLE 9.2 Performance of Largest Bank Loan Mutual Funds

| Top 5 Funds | AUM ($B) | Annualized Total Returns as of 12/31/14 | | | Fees | |
		1-Yr	3-Yr	5-Yr	Total Operating Expenses	Initial / Deferred
Benchmark: S&P/LSTA Lev Perf Loan Index	$748.6	1.8%	5.6%	5.7%	–	–
Oppenheimer Sen Floating Rate	$17.3	0.6%	5.1%	6.1%	1.0%	3.5%
Fidelity Floating Rate High Income	$13.2	0.4%	3.7%	4.1%	0.7%	0.0%*
Eaton Vance Floating Rate Fund	$10.5	0.3%	4.3%	4.8%	1.0%	2.3%
Lord Abbett Floating Rate Fund	$6.8	0.9%	5.6%	5.2%	0.8%	2.3%
RidgeWorth Floating Rate High Income	$6.5	0.5%	4.7%	5.0%	0.9%	2.5%

Note: As of December 31, 2014. *Sales fees of 1.0% only apply within a 0–60 redemption period.
Source: Morningstar, S&P Capital IQ LCD

managers: (1) often maintain a sizeable cash reserve, particularly in times of stress, (2) have some portion of their holdings in corporate bonds which settle faster, and (3) often have a credit facility in place to use in times of need. Understanding how well the fund is set up to manage redemptions in illiquid markets is an important consideration when investing in an open-end leveraged loan or "bank loan" fund.

Table 9.2 lists the top leveraged loan mutual funds by size. Of the leveraged loan funds listed, Oppenheimer is the largest with almost $19 billion of AUM at year-end 2014. Similar to bond mutual funds, the sales load fees for bank loan mutual funds can be significant, especially for smaller investors. For example, Oppenheimer's senior floating rate fund charges a 3.5% sales load for investments less than $100,000. These fees scale down to 1.5% for investments between $500,000 to $1,000,000 and are less for investments of $1,000,000 or greater. A smaller investor might find the Fidelity Floating Rate High Income fund a better choice, which operates with a lower operating expense and has a lower sales load charge.

9.3 HIGH YIELD ETFs

The first high yield bond ETF was introduced in 2007, and since then ETFs have grown in popularity due to their liquidity and low-cost structure. At year-end 2014, there were over 15 high yield ETFs that collectively managed $37 billion of AUM.[2] High yield ETFs operate like open-end mutual funds that create and redeem shares at the NAV. However, unlike mutual funds, ETF shares are traded on a national exchange and therefore offer intra-day liquidity. In declining or rising markets, this allows investors to react more quickly to take advantage of market conditions. ETFs have no sales loads or upfront fees, operate with low expense structure, and trade at values close to the fund's NAV. For investors with a shorter term investment horizon, ETFs provide a means to gain high yield exposure cost-efficiently.

High yield ETFs track different high yield indices and this can explain differences in performance. When evaluating an ETF, review the holdings by rating category and maturity to understand what risk an ETF like the iShares iBoxx $ High Yield Corporate Bond (ticker: HYG) poses in relation to the SPDR Barclays High Yield Bond (ticker: JNK). JNK tends to hold more lower rated debt as a percentage of its total portfolio in comparison to HYG.

ETFs can be scaled because they seek to replicate an index. At the time of writing this, HYG, the largest high yield ETF, had over 1,000 holdings and $13 billion of assets. This implies an average position in the underlying high yield issues of $13 million. Most of the debt issues HYG buys are in $1 billion plus debt tranches. As such, scaling up and down in individual positions is not so much of a challenge for a high yield ETF. The size of an investment strategy matters more with actively managed funds that seek to gain specific types of high yield exposure. These types of funds may lose some capacity to outperform benchmarks when they get too large.

A common concern raised with high yield ETFs is that they may not be able to sell holdings in extremely stressed and illiquid markets and this could result in a tracking error to the index. In markets where high yield liquidity becomes severely constrained, like in 2008, share redemption and creation can become difficult and this illiquidity can cause a high yield ETF's shares to trade at a discount to NAV. Remove that environment and

---

[2]Lipper FMI.

a high yield ETF is set up in a way that permits it to function efficiently for a few reasons. First, high yield ETFs are allowed to operate with some tracking error, substituting holdings when one cannot be easily sourced. This allows for greater operational flexibility. Second, a high yield ETF like HYG is highly diversified in its holdings, more so than most mutual funds. This provides a broader opportunity set to both buy and liquidate. Last, an investor redeeming an interest does not necessarily necessitate changes in the ETFs holdings. An ETF's shares can be bought and sold by other investors in the secondary market.

Another concern commonly raised with high yield ETFs is their potential to exacerbate market volatility. The rationale behind this concern is that as high yield ETFs have grown in size so has their influence on market trading. It is true that the growth in the number and size of high yield ETFs does create more potential for market volatility because the capital that goes into these funds can be redeemed rather quickly. Further, if a high yield ETF seeks to liquidate assets in a down market, it can force price discovery on illiquid issues that drive down market prices further. But it's important to keep in mind that ETFs still represent a small fraction of the overall market and secondary trading volume. HYG and JNK alone at the time of writing represent only 1.5% of the total high yield bond market. Therefore, it's not yet the case that ETFs capital flows are driving overall market trends.

Table 9.3 compares the performance of various high yield bonds ETFs to a high yield bond index. An ETF provides a cost-effective means to gain broad-based asset class exposure. Mutual funds and other actively managed strategies in contrast employ more credit selection to find debt issues with attractive risk-return attributes. Depending on the market environment, each investment approach can have its merits. For example, coming out of a recession with prices still low could justify a more diversified, asset class approach. A case for active management can be made later in the credit cycle, when performance differences between different high yield segments start to manifest.

Bank loan ETFs operate with a similar settlement mismatch as bank loan mutual funds. Funds like ticker: BKLN, the largest bank loan ETF, have defensive mechanisms in place to protect against this withdrawal risk including holding a cash position, investing a portion of the portfolio in bonds that settle at T+3 days, and maintaining an undrawn credit facility that could be used in more extreme scenarios. With these protections in place, BKLN seems well positioned to meet redemption even in more

TABLE 9.3   Performance of Largest High Yield Bond ETFs

Top 5 Funds	AUM ($B)	Annualized NAV Return as of 12/31/14			Annualized Price Return as of 12/31/14			Total Operating Expenses
		1-Yr	3-Yr	5-Yr	1-Yr	3-Yr	5-Yr	
Benchmark: JPM US High Yield Index	$788.9	2.2%	8.5%	9.4%	–	–	–	–
iShares iBoxx $ High Yield Corporate Bond	$14.4	2.0%	7.1%	7.8%	1.9%	6.4%	7.5%	0.5%
SPDR Barclays High Yield Bond	$9.7	1.2%	7.0%	7.9%	0.8%	6.6%	7.8%	0.4%
SPDR Barclays Short Term High Yield	$3.9	−0.7%	NA	NA	−1.3%	NA	NA	0.4%
PIMCO 0-5 Year High Yield Corp	$2.9	0.5%	6.9%	NA	−0.1%	6.2%	NA	0.6%
Guggenheim BulletShrs 2015 HY Corp	$1.0	1.6%	6.4%	NA	0.4%	5.7%	NA	0.4%

Note: As of December 31, 2014.
Source: Morningstar, J.P. Morgan

price volatile environments. A concern though might be to what extent these defensive mechanisms detract from performance.

Table 9.4 lists performance of the top bank loan ETFs in comparison to a leveraged loan index. Similar to high yield bond ETFs, these funds can be actively or passively managed. Most funds today have limited operating history given how new the ETF structure is for high yield.

One thing to note, when evaluating any fund it is important to always obtain information directly from the fund manager, as other sources of information may not be up to date. As an example, at the time of writing this, BKLN was listed on Bloomberg as having less than 1% of its assets in cash holdings when in fact it had 8%. Due to the mismatch in timing between bank loan settlements and share redemptions, this is a significant consideration.

TABLE 9.4 Performance of Largest Bank Loan ETFs

Top 4 Funds	AUM ($B)	Annualized NAV Return as of 12/31/14			Annualized Price Return as of 12/31/14			Total Operating Expenses
		1-Yr	3-Yr	5-Yr	1-Yr	3-Yr	5-Yr	
Benchmark: S&P/LSTA Lev Loan 100 Index	$252.3	1.0%	5.4%	5.3%	–	–	–	0.0%
PowerShares Senior Loan	$5.7	0.7%	5.0%	NA	0.5%	4.8%	NA	0.7%
SPDR Blackstone / GSO Senior Loan	$0.6	0.9%	NA	NA	1.0%	NA	NA	0.7%
Highland/iBoxx Senior Loan	$0.3	0.7%	NA	NA	0.6%	NA	NA	0.6%
First Trust Senior Loan	$0.2	1.9%	NA	NA	1.4%	NA	NA	0.9%

Note: As of December 31, 2014.
Source: Morningstar, S&P Capital IQ LCD

9.4 HIGH YIELD CLOSED-END FUNDS

Closed-end funds sell a fixed number of shares that are listed and trade on a national stock exchange. They then use this capital to buy a portfolio of high yield debt, which can be diversified or more concentrated. Unlike open-end funds, closed-end funds do not redeem or create shares from investors directly. If an investor wants to sell or buy shares, they must do so on the secondary market. For this reason, closed-end funds often trade at a premium or discount to NAV based on market demand for the stock.

Closed-end funds benefit from not having to manage their investment portfolio for liquidity. This allows funds to be more fully invested, with less cash reserves, and to buy more illiquid debt instruments with higher risk premium. It also allows the funds to more easily employ leverage. From a fee standpoint, closed-end funds are generally more expensive than ETFs and less expensive than open-end mutual funds. When deciding whether to invest in a closed-end fund, a primary consideration is that share price performance can deviate from NAV performance. For example, the NAV could appreciate while the share prices declines, causing the stock to trade

TABLE 9.5   Performance of Largest High Yield Bond Closed-End Funds

Top 5 Funds	Market Cap ($B)	Annualized NAV Return as of 12/31/14			Annualized Price Return as of 12/31/14			Total Operating Expenses	Premium / Discount
		1-Yr	3-Yr	5-Yr	1-Yr	3-Yr	5-Yr		
Benchmark: JPM US High Yield Index	$788.9	2.2%	8.5%	9.4%	–	–	–	–	–
BlackRock Corp High Yield	$1.6	3.6%	12.4%	11.9%	2.2%	9.3%	10.9%	1.3%	−8.6%
AllianceBernstein Glb High	$1.2	3.7%	10.5%	10.4%	−3.0%	5.9%	9.1%	1.0%	−11.2%
BlackRock Debt Strategies Fund	$0.8	2.6%	9.7%	10.2%	0.5%	6.7%	9.2%	1.2%	−11.2%
Western Asset High Inc Fund II	$0.7	−1.1%	11.0%	11.0%	1.0%	5.0%	8.8%	1.4%	−1.8%
Prudential Global Short Dur Hi	$0.7	0.6%	NA	NA	1.9%	NA	NA	1.6%	−7.3%

Note: As of December 31, 2014.
Source: Morningstar, J.P. Morgan

at a discount to NAV. This could persist for some time and make exiting the position costly. For this reason, it's important to consider whether a closed-end fund is trading at a premium or discount to NAV and the likelihood for that to change.

The top five high yield bond closed-end funds, listed in Table 9.5, are smaller than the top mutual fund or ETF products. When compared to the JPM US High Yield index, most of these funds have performed well over time. Investors that have a longer term investment horizon and are less concerned with liquidity should consider buying closed-end funds when they are trading at a discount to NAV. This sometimes occurs when supply and demand imbalances put the high yield asset class out of favor.

The liquidity profile of closed-end funds makes them a more natural buyer of leveraged loans. Due to the closed-end structure, settlement differences matter less and capital can therefore be more fully deployed into income earning assets. Table 9.6 lists the top five closed-end bank loan funds by AUM. The returns illustrate how leverage can improve performance versus the benchmark and the premium/discount shows how

TABLE 9.6 Performance of the Largest Bank Loan Closed-End Funds

Top 5 Funds	Market Cap ($B)	Annualized NAV Return as of 12/31/14			Annualized Price Return as of 12/31/14			Total Operating Expenses	Premium / Discount
		1-Yr	3-Yr	5-Yr	1-Yr	3-Yr	5-Yr		
Benchmark: S&P/LSTA Lev Perf Loan Index	$748.6	1.8%	5.6%	5.7%	–	–	–	–	–
Nuveen Credit Strategies Income Fund	$1.4	3.1%	10.4%	9.9%	–4.1%	10.9%	11.2%	2.0%	–12.1%
Invesco VK Dynamic Cred Opps	$1.0	2.6%	10.9%	8.7%	–1.3%	11.6%	7.9%	2.3%	–10.0%
Invesco Senior Income	$0.9	2.0%	9.0%	8.9%	–3.3%	9.3%	8.5%	2.2%	–9.2%
Voya Prime Rate Trust	$0.9	2.3%	8.3%	7.2%	–2.9%	8.5%	6.9%	2.1%	–8.8%
Nuveen Floating Rate Fund	$0.7	1.0%	9.6%	8.8%	–1.9%	7.7%	8.4%	2.3%	–9.1%

Note: As of December 31, 2014.
Source: Morningstar, S&P Capital IQ LCD

significantly share prices can deviate from NAV. If an investor has a longer term investment horizon and was less concerned about liquidity, buying a well-managed closed-end fund at a discount could present an excellent means to gain leveraged loan exposure.

9.5 COMPARISON OF CLOSED-END AND OPEN-END FUND RETURNS

Table 9.7 compares the performance from 2004–2014 of the largest closed-end and open-end funds based on assets under management at year-end 2014. The ability to trade at a premium to NAV as well as more easily employ fund leverage allowed closed-end funds to outperform open-end funds in most years when market returns were strong. In years where the market was negative or posted modest gains, open-end funds tended to fare better.

TABLE 9.7   Comparison of Closed-End versus Open-End Fund Returns

Year	Closed-End HY Bond Fund			Open-End HY Bond Fund	JPM US High Yield Index
	BlackRock Corp High Yield			American Funds High-Income Trust	
	Price Return	NAV Return	Prem / Discount	NAV Return	
2014	2.2%	3.6%	−8.6%	0.5%	2.2%
2013	7.3%	12.3%	−6.5%	6.4%	8.2%
2012	19.2%	22.0%	−1.7%	14.5%	15.4%
2011	6.9%	3.3%	0.6%	2.0%	7.0%
2010	20.1%	19.5%	−2.5%	15.0%	14.7%
2009	92.6%	80.7%	−2.7%	48.4%	58.2%
2008	−38.4%	−42.2%	−8.2%	−27.5%	−26.6%
2007	−2.1%	0.2%	−12.0%	1.5%	2.6%
2006	17.9%	11.3%	−9.0%	12.2%	11.6%
2005	−5.3%	1.1%	−13.3%	3.6%	2.4%
2004	15.5%	15.5%	−6.1%	9.8%	11.1%

Note: As of December 31, 2014.
Source: Morningstar, J.P. Morgan

Table 9.8 shows this same analysis for the largest closed-end and open-end bank loan funds at year-end 2014. The conclusion is similar and highlights the opportunity with closed-end funds when they are trading at a deep discount to NAV and the greater return stability of open-end funds when the market outlook is more uncertain.

9.6   BUSINESS DEVELOPMENT COMPANIES

Business development companies (BDCs) are closed-end funds that were established to provide financing to small and mid-sized U.S. businesses but, over the years, have greatly expanded their investment activities. This form of company was created by Congress in 1980 as an amendment to the Investment Company Act of 1940. One advantage of the BDC structure is that it allows non-accredited investors, or investors that don't meet income, net worth or other requirements, to gain exposure to private financings in earlier stage companies. BDCs often buy privately placed debt issues in companies too small to access the syndicated high yield market. This type of debt, which is more illiquid, is not typically held by other 1940 Act funds

TABLE 9.8 Comparison of Closed-End versus Open-End Fund Returns

Year	Closed-End Bank Loan Fund			Open-End Bank Loan Fund	S&P LSTA Leveraged Loan Index
	Nuveen Credit Strategies Income Fund			Oppenheimer Sen. Floating Rate	
	Price Return	NAV Return	Prem / Discount	NAV Return	
2014	−4.1%	3.1%	−12.1%	0.6%	1.6%
2013	8.9%	11.7%	−5.0%	6.4%	5.3%
2012	30.6%	16.9%	−2.3%	8.4%	9.7%
2011	0.3%	−1.7%	−12.3%	2.4%	1.5%
2010	24.4%	21.1%	−13.1%	13.2%	10.1%
2009	78.6%	64.2%	−14.6%	43.5%	51.6%
2008	−49.3%	−46.1%	−19.4%	−29.5%	−29.1%
2007	−14.7%	−5.3%	−11.7%	1.5%	2.0%
2006	26.8%	8.8%	−1.3%	7.1%	6.8%
2005	−3.8%	1.6%	−14.7%	5.6%	5.1%
2004	3.0%	10.4%	−8.8%	7.2%	5.2%

Note: As of December 31, 2014.
Source: Morningstar, S&P Capital IQ LCD

TABLE 9.9 Performance of Largest Business Development Companies

Top 5 Funds	Market Cap ($B)	Annualized Total Returns as of 12/31/14			Dividend Yield	Premium/ Discount
		1-Yr	3-Yr	5-Yr		
Benchmark: S&P/LSTA Lev Perf Loan Index	$748.6	1.8%	5.6%	5.7%	–	–
Ares Capital Corp.	$4.9	−3.4%	9.7%	14.1%	10.4%	−7.2%
American Capital, Ltd	$3.9	−6.6%	29.5%	43.0%	NM	−28.0%
Prospect Capital Corp.	$3.0	−14.6%	8.7%	4.7%	16.1%	−21.5%
Apollo Investment Corp.	$1.8	−3.0%	15.2%	6.0%	10.8%	−12.0%
Fifth Street Finance Corp.	$1.2	−2.2%	5.5%	5.2%	12.9%	−12.6%

Note: As of December 31, 2014.
Source: Morningstar, S&P Capital IQ LCD

and is instead held by private mezzanine funds, which are only available to accredited investors.

The market for BDCs has grown significantly over the years. At year-end 2014, there were over 60 BDCs accounting for approximately $60 billion of assets operating in three different formats: traded BDCs, non-traded BDCs, and private BDCs.[3] Over 50 of the BDCs were traded BDCs that sell shares to the public and are listed and traded on a national exchange like NASDAQ or NYSE similar to other closed-end funds. Thirteen were so-called non-traded BDCs, or BDCs that sell shares privately and offer investors liquidity through periodic repurchase offers until the company decides to launch a traditional IPO, typically some years later. Non-traded BDCs offer investors the potential for lower price volatility, as the shares are not publicly traded, while maintaining the upside of pre-IPO investing. Private BDCs are a relatively recent development and are relatively rare. In this structure, shares are sold through a private placement and investment funding is effectuated via a capital call model similar to how other private investment funds operate.

BDCs differ from other 1940 Act funds in several important ways. First, BDCs are more often involved with directly originating financings versus buying syndicated offerings. This allows for more differentiated high yield exposure often to smaller and mid-sized companies. Second, BDCs can use leverage so long as they have 200% asset coverage; this means they can borrow $1 of debt for every $1 of equity, which is higher leverage than other 1940 Act funds are allowed to employ. Third, BDCs often have more concentrated investment portfolios in illiquid investments. Since BDCs raise permanent capital through an IPO, they have flexibility to make higher returning investments that are less liquid.

The fee structures of BDCs are more closely aligned with private equity or hedge funds, where they charge an annual management fee of generally 1.5%–2.0% and a performance fee, which can amount to 20% of the profits above a certain pre-determined hurdle. Intended to be an income stock, BDCs typically provide a quarterly dividend to investors, which can be quite substantial. Fund managers work hard to sustain and improve the dividend over time. But to support dividends and cover management and performance fees, investments often must generate double digit returns,

---

[3]Sutherland Asbill & Brennan LLP.

and capital losses must be kept to a minimum. This can be challenging to achieve consistently, particularly in lower yield environments.

When evaluating a BDC it is important to understand the sustainability of the dividend. This can be assessed by understanding the sources of income and to what extent cash earnings cover projected dividend payments. The next area of focus is on the assets. Like other closed-end funds, BDCs can trade at a premium and discount to NAV. Unlike other closed-end funds that invest in syndicated offerings that are widely traded, many BDCs holdings will not have active quotes because they are not traded debt with a clearly established market value. Understanding whether these assets are fairly valued or have potential for impairment is important to assessing the BDC's earning potential and the quality of the NAV. Last, it's important to understand the strategy and how it differs from other BDCs. Some BDCs have expertise in sourcing and originating transactions within a certain market segment or industry. This can provide advantages in creating more attractive and differentiated high yield exposure. Others can provide exposure to areas like CLO equity or unitranches, which are difficult to gain access to through other fund structures.

9.7 SUMMARY

Over time, more 1940 Act funds have been introduced to capitalize on retail demand for high yield debt. Chapter 9 provides an overview of the pros and cons of each fund structure. Mutual funds provide the benefit of active management, which needs to be weighed against their fee structure. The largest ETFs are cost-efficient but take a passive approach toward investing and focus on replicating index returns. Closed-end funds can operate more optimally without having to meet daily redemptions or be concerned with settlement issues, but these funds can be more illiquid and trade at a discount to NAV. That sometimes presents an opportunity for longer term investors. BDCs provide a completely different type of high yield exposure in more privately originated transactions. While these funds charge higher fees and can be difficult to perform due diligence on, they can offer attractive dividend yields and more capital appreciation potential.

CHAPTER 10

Mezzanine Debt, Distressed Debt, and Credit Hedge Funds

C hapter 10 provides an overview of three types of private funds that invest in the high yield market. Unlike 1940 Act funds, mezzanine debt, distressed debt, and credit hedge funds are not publicly registered with the SEC and are not available to the general public. Instead, they are private partnerships that buy higher yielding, oftentimes more illiquid, investments to enhance risk-adjusted returns. Intended for high net worth individuals and institutional investors, private debt funds provide an opportunity to potentially generate higher investment returns from the high yield asset class through more concentrated and actively managed investment strategies.

10.1 PRIVATE INVESTMENT FUNDS

Most private investment funds are set up as limited partnerships that raise capital from a broad group of investors including pension funds, foundations, endowments, insurance companies, institutional investors, and high net worth individuals. Unlike 1940 Act funds, private funds are exempt from certain regulations which allows them to operate more flexible investment strategies. For instance, private funds can sell shares short, something mutual funds cannot do, they have no limitation on the use of leverage, whereas mutual funds cannot have more than one-third of their total assets financed with debt. Another key difference between private and public funds relate to liquidity. Closed-end private investment funds operate without any redemption rights. If an investor wants to sell its interest, it must find another investor willing to buy its ownership stake or wait until the term ends. Others operate similarly to open-end funds with capital that can be added or redeemed periodically at the NAV, typically quarterly or semi-annually.

Private investment funds can only be sold to individuals and institutions that meet certain net worth and income requirements. To participate in a private investment fund, also known as an "alternative" fund, an individual or institution typically must be both an accredited investor and qualified purchaser, depending on how the fund is set up. There are tests that define whether one qualifies as an accredited investor or qualified purchaser. For example, at the time of writing an accredited investor is an individual who had income in each of the two most recent years in excess of $200,000, joint annual income with the investor's spouse in excess of $300,000, or net worth in excess of $1,000,000 (excluding primary residence). For business entities, total assets must exceed $5,000,000. The definition of qualified purchaser sets a higher standard. Individuals are required to own no less than $5,000,000 of investments in financial instruments; companies must have $25 million invested in financial instruments. These provisions are intended to safeguard investors with fewer resources from making fund investments that might later prove financially hazardous.

In order to be exempt from the registration requirements and strategy limitations of the Investment Company Act of 1940, private investment funds rely on Section 3(c)(1) or Section 3(c)(7) of the 1940 Act. The most practical consideration of each of these exemptions relates to the number and type of investors the private investment fund can accept. Funds that are exempt under Section 3(c)(1) may not be owned by more than 100 investors. Funds exempt under Section 3(c)(7) can only be offered and sold to qualified purchasers. Another practical consideration is that funds operating under these exemptions are precluded from publicly offering their shares.

In exchange for greater management expertise and the potential for outsized returns, private investment funds charge higher fees than most 1940 Act funds. A typical private fund for example will have a management fee, charged annually on assets under management, of 1.0%–2.0%, and a performance fee, which is calculated on profits and ranges from 10%–20%. The performance fee is often subject to a *hurdle,* or minimum return that must be achieved which might be 5%–7%, or a *high water mark*, which ensures a fund manager does not get paid for negative performance and serves as an investor protection. A high water mark requires assets that decline in value to reach their previous peak value before additional performance fees (also called *carry* or *incentive fees*) can be paid. For example, if a high net worth individual invests $1,000,000 on January 1, 2015 and experiences a 3% decline in the first month, the fund will have to recover lost value and grow before it can earn any performance fees subject to a high water mark.

There are three types of alternative funds that provide high yield exposure. This includes mezzanine debt funds, distressed debt funds, and credit hedge funds. Each of these funds operates with a unique investment approach that differs from each other as well as more traditional 1940 Act funds. The following pages explain the characteristics of each fund type.

10.2 MEZZANINE DEBT FUNDS

Mezzanine debt funds were historically funds that provided debt financing to companies that were either too small or complex for the syndicated high yield market. Oftentimes, this was structured as senior subordinated debt, which is a form of debt junior in right of payment to senior secured debt and senior to equity capital. Layered in the middle of the capital structure – this type of financing at some point took on the name "mezzanine." Mezzanine debt funds generally seek to generate 10%–15% returns from investments. The high rate of return is generated through upfront fees, interest income, call protection, and equity co-investments.

When a mezzanine fund invests in a company they are often the only holder or one of a few holders of that debt. If developments occur that cause the company to underperform, reducing exposure in the debt by selling down is difficult. As a result, most mezzanine funds conduct substantial due diligence prior to making an investment and seek to hold investments for the long term. In comparison to investments in syndicated offerings, mezzanine funds are generally granted access to significantly more information to reach their decision. In order to make the types of investments where a mezzanine fund finds value, it must have committed capital that is locked up for the life of the investment as selling is not an easy option. Most harvests, or repayments of the investment, occur when the issuer is sold to another buyer or can refinance its debt. The debt rarely remains outstanding until maturity.

In the 1990s, the mezzanine finance industry consisted primarily of smaller funds financing small-cap issuers. At the time, the high yield market was less open to smaller issuers and a second lien market, which provides smaller sized junior loans, did not exist in any meaningful way. Goldman Sachs, Blackstone, and TCW were among the pioneers that transformed the industry to meet the need for subordinated debt capital. Sometime around the year 2000, these asset managers raised larger mezzanine funds that could support mid-cap issuers. Some of the early financings from these funds had mid-teen interest rates and could even carry warrants, a term that is nearly forgotten today. *Warrants* are issued by a company and give the holder the right to buy equity shares at a specific price within a certain time frame. Penny warrants were often issued in connection with mezzanine financings and these had a de minimis cost to exercise but could provide significant upside to potential returns if the company proved successful.

The mezzanine finance industry has experienced tremendous growth over the years and mezzanine funds today provide exposure to issuers in the United States, Europe, and other places in the world. However, developments in the high yield bond and leveraged loan markets have provided more opportunities for smaller issuers to raise capital through syndicated offerings. In particular, the second lien loan market, which typically offers issuers capital at a lower cost than mezzanine funds, has also grown, at the expense of mezzanine funds.

Mezzanine funds have adapted to these challenges by offering more creative capital structure solutions and providing certainty of capital. Since a mezzanine fund draws from committed capital, it is not affected by swings in the market that affect the broader capital markets. Capital certainty is valued most during periods of volatility or at times when the capital markets become more difficult to access; this is often when the best investment opportunities arise. Mezzanine funds can also distinguish themselves by their ability to due diligence complex situations and source attractive risk-reward as a result. They sometimes have industry expertise that allows them to invest in situations that are not straightforward opportunities for others with less know-how and experience.

Success of the mezzanine fund's investment strategy ultimately depends on the skills of the fund manager to source and make good investments. When investments underperform, managers need to be prepared to restructure balance sheets, invest new capital, and own businesses through a recovery if necessary and sensible. But success can also relate to careful portfolio composition. Because of the time it takes to source and make private investments, mezzanine funds may have portfolios that consist of only 15–20 positions. The illiquidity of mezzanine positions makes managing losses difficult for mezzanine funds and portfolio concentration makes these losses more detrimental to overall fund returns. To offset inevitable losses, a mezzanine fund will try to invest some portion of the fund in the equity of the companies it provides debt financing to. This is usually done in some ratio such as 1:10 (e.g., $5 million of equity on a $50 million debt investment). Equity provides the potential for meaningful capital appreciation should the company perform and the debt get called early. When investing in mezzanine funds, it's critical to understand the track record of the manager, their sourcing network, diligence expertise, and portfolio construction philosophy.

10.3   DISTRESSED DEBT FUNDS

Distressed debt is a term that refers to debt that is trading 1,000 bps over the risk-free rate or for less than 75–80 cents on the dollar. There is no perfect or universally agreed-upon definition for distressed debt however, especially because in 2008 many performing credits traded at these levels. What makes debt "distressed" is not just defined by price or yield but relates more fundamentally to financial duress that the issuer is, or is expected to experience. Loans and bonds become distressed for a number of reasons including a slowdown in the economy or recession, loss of a key customer, decline in commodity prices, material change in cost structure or end-market demand, or secular shifts like what happened when the publishing industry moved from print to digital. Companies that are distressed have over-leveraged capital structures and management teams and owners that sometimes have made poor decisions.

As debt declines in price to distressed levels, the holders of that debt turn over. Investors that favor performing credits, sell; investors that see opportunity in turmoil, buy. Distressed debt funds fall into this latter camp; they operate a business model that is a hybrid between debt and private equity investing. Distress debt funds amass positions at steep discounts to par in an effort to create equity-like returns. There are a variety of distressed debt investment strategies. Some strategies are more passive with the expectation of some catalyst occurring that will create value. Others are more active and involve litigating claims to obtain a recovery. In the high yield market, the largest distressed debt funds manage billions of dollars and often aspire to control or own a distressed company through a restructuring process where the debt gets exchanged for equity. To do this, the distressed debt funds are generally prepared to provide debtor-in-possession (DIP) financings, facilitate in-court and out-of-court restructurings with additional capital, and orchestrate debt exchanges. Essentially, these are all distressed debt tactics used by one class of creditors to exert influence over another.

Some distressed debt funds operate with long-term committed capital; others are funds that allow investors to redeem periodically. The nature of this capital affects the type of risks that can be taken, specifically with liquidity. Funds that allow for redemptions tend to buy somewhat liquid claims, like the debt claims of AIG or Lehman Brothers after they became distressed, and seek some catalyst for price appreciation. Funds with committed capital are more focused on long-term gain and care less about liquidity. As it relates to evaluating distressed funds, the overall market environment is a major consideration. In periods of economic growth and low default rates, there can be a lot of distressed funds focusing on few distressed opportunities, which leads to frothy valuations. For this reason, many distressed fund managers are skilled at looking at a variety of markets to create a broad opportunity set. When markets and the economy take a turn for the worse, distressed funds can be the prime beneficiaries and create attractive, uncorrelated returns compared to more traditional long positions.

10.4 CREDIT HEDGE FUNDS

Credit hedge funds employ a broad range of investment strategies which can make them confusing to understand. Unlike 1940 Act funds, which cannot short, hedge funds seek to make profits through both long and short positions and often employ substantial leverage to enhance returns. Long positions are traditional investments where a loan, security, or some other product is bought with the expectation that the asset will rise in value. Short positions refer to the sale of a borrowed asset with the expectation that it will fall in value. Financing a short high yield position requires not only paying for the "borrow" or securities that are lent but also paying the interest on the debt sold short. This makes shorting high yield debt expensive, particularly over long time periods.

The investment strategies hedge funds employ are wide ranging. Long/short funds buy assets they believe are undervalued and short assets they think are overvalued. In this strategy, the long book could be larger than the short book. Market neutral strategies employ a similar long/short approach to investing but try to achieve a beta as close to zero as possible to protect against general market risk. These types of funds are intended to limit downside exposure but can also have limited upside in rising markets. Fixed income arbitrage involves exploiting price differences between fixed income securities. There are a variety of ways managers seek to profit through this strategy including by taking long and short positions in Treasuries of various maturities or exploiting price differences between synthetic indices like CDX and other markets.

One type of fixed income arbitrage often employed with high yield is capital structure arbitrage. Capital structure arbitrage relates to profiting from pricing differentials between senior and junior securities of the same issuer. For example, debt that is overvalued might be shorted to buy another debt claim or company stock that looks relatively cheap.

Credit hedge funds may also be long or short biased. A short-biased high yield focused credit hedge fund might forecast losses in constant or improving markets due to the cost of shorting bonds but could provide big pay-offs in downside scenarios and thereby serve as a portfolio hedge in the context of a larger fixed income portfolio. A long-biased credit hedge fund might have little or no short exposure.

Another popular strategy is event-driven investing. This is an investing strategy that seeks to exploit pricing inefficiencies that may occur before or after events like a bankruptcy, merger, or spin-off. For example, if a company is expected to go bankrupt, an event-driven investor might buy senior claims trading at a discount and short equity or junior debt claims that will experience a low recovery. The success of a credit hedge fund ultimately relates to its ability to generate alpha, or excess return, from long positions that appreciate and short positions that depreciate in value.

With high yield debt, there are three primary ways fund managers obtain short exposure. The most traditional means is to short bonds with the expectation that some catalyst (e.g., an earnings release or bankruptcy) will cause the bonds to decline in price. Another way to short high yield is to use options on high yield ETFs or other correlated equities. An option strategy might entail buying puts or put spreads on HYG, JNK and BKLN. All of these ETFs have an active options market with HYG being the largest. Credit default swaps (CDS) is another instrument that provides short exposure. CDS exist for many high yield issuers as well as indices including high yield and investment grade. A long position in CDX, which is based on a basket of single issuer CDS, acts like insurance with period payments made that provide profit potential when credit risks develop.

A credit hedge fund model provides fund managers with flexibility to consider how best to express views through the use of long positions, short positions, derivatives, and options. When evaluating credit hedge funds focused on high yield debt, it's important to understand how much leverage and hedging is employed and how the fund can perform in varying stressed scenarios. It's difficult for any fund to consistently generate high returns while also providing comprehensive downside protection. Shorting and hedges are expensive and detract from returns when markets go up. If a fund consistently hedges but produces lower returns, it ought to have a higher Sharpe ratio, which is a metric that tracks volatility adjusted returns. When investing in hedge funds, allocators must sometimes choose between high returns with more volatility or lower returns with more consistency. Not all funds will produce either, but diligence can help surface what you're in for.

10.5 SUMMARY

Mezzanine debt, distressed debt, and credit hedge funds constitute the three types of private funds that operate in the high yield market. Mezzanine funds can provide exposure to an entirely different high yield market segment, which consists of smaller issuers. These funds can also capitalize on market volatility with more committed, long-term capital. Distressed debt funds can be highly profitable when the economy does not perform well and default risk spikes. This is usually a time when other portfolio holdings decline in value, which makes these funds a useful portfolio complement. Credit hedge funds operate with a broader mandate and can take advantage of both declining and appreciating markets through short and long investment strategies. There are many credit hedge funds that invest in both high yield bonds and leveraged loans, often owning lower rated, higher returning debt. These funds are willing to expend time and resources to understand difficult and complex situations that other investors may shun. When companies underperform or the markets sell-off, credit hedge funds are able to profit from declines and mitigate the losses of a long-only portfolio, such as those held by 1940 Act funds would sustain.

This benefit must be weighed against a more concentrated portfolio of potentially higher risk assets and greater use of leverage, which may outweigh the benefits of mandate flexibility. SEC regulation is effectively set up to limit the use of these investment vehicles to sophisticated investors who can grasp the risks and have the financial resources to withstand the possibility of loss that comes with the potential for higher returns.

Glossary

144A offering with registration rights   Refers to a debt offering that is initially sold via Rule 144A (see below) but where the issuer agrees to file public statements at a later date, usually 180–540 days following the initial offering. Owners of the 144A-issued bonds can exchange their bonds for registered notes to make those bonds publicly tradable.

Accelerate   When debt holders declare their debt due and payable following an event of default.

Additional debt   A provision that refers to the accordion or incremental facilities in the context of leveraged loans and additional notes in the context of high yield bonds.

Affirmative covenants   Outline actions an issuer must take in the ordinary course, such as comply with taxes, maintain insurance, provide certain financial information, and maintain books and records.

AHYDO (Applicable High Yield Discount Obligations)   Refers to tax rules that defer or disallow tax deductions for interest on debt that resembles equity finance.

Ask   Refers to the price at which a security or other financial instrument can be sold (e.g., the asking price).

Asset-based loan   A type of revolving credit facility, or capital line that provides the issuer with the ability to draw-down and repay capital based on its needs, but with eligibility based on an advance rate to certain assets, such as accounts receivable and inventory.

Bank book   A type of offering memorandum for leveraged loans. The bank book is also referred to as a confidential information memorandum (CIM). See Offering memorandum.

Basis points   Changes in interest rates and credit spreads are often stated in basis points (bps). One basis point (bp) equals 1/100th of 1.0% or 0.01%. 100 bps equals 1.0%.

Baskets   Refers to exceptions to the negative covenants. A company might have a $100 million basket to raise additional debt but otherwise be prohibited from doing so. Baskets are often limited by a dollar amount or pro forma ratio.

Below investment grade   A term used by rating agencies that refers to debt rated below BBB-/Baa3. Speculative grade, below investment grade, and high yield are all terms used interchangeably.

Benchmark hugger   See Index hugger.

Best efforts   In a best efforts syndication, the investment bank does not underwrite the debt offering but rather uses its "best efforts" to sell the debt offering. If the offering does not sell, the investment bank has no obligation to provide any capital to the issuer. Best efforts syndications often occur with more opportunistic or questionable transactions where demand and the probability of success are less certain.

Beta   Calculated using a regression analysis and quantifies the volatility of a security or index in relation to another.

Bid   Refers to the price at which a security or other financial instrument can be bought (e.g., the bid price).

Borrowing base   The amount of capital available to a company based on advance rates against eligible assets. If a lender is willing to provide a company a capital line based on its accounts receivable and inventory, the borrowing base would take into account the amount of those assets less any applicable haircuts.

Building baskets   Baskets that "build" over the years by the percentage of cumulative net income or cash flow earned by the issuer. The amount accumulated in a building basket can only be used if the issuer could "incur $1 of debt," and still be in compliance with a ratio test such as the 2:1 interest coverage test.

Bullet maturity   A type of debt maturity where the entire outstanding amount is paid at maturity. High yield bonds have bullet maturities while many leveraged loans contain amortization and excess cash flow sweep requirements that force some early repayment.

Call protection   A provision that prevents an issuer from calling, or redeeming, a debt instrument early. High yield bonds often have onerous call protection provisions which make it expensive for issuers to repay this debt early. This ensures the bond offers a minimum duration or dollar profit. Loans have less call protection and therefore can more easily be repaid.

Capital structure   The mix of debt and equity that a company has outstanding. It reflects the capital that finances a company's overall operations or the capital mix used to facilitate a buyout. The capital structures for leveraged buyouts, for example, often consist of leveraged loans, high yield bonds, and private equity.

Carry fee   A performance fee charged to an investor in a private investment fund, typically between 10%–20% of the profits. This is also called an incentive fee.

Carve-outs   A term similar to basket and referring to an exception to the negative covenants. While baskets refer to amounts, carve-outs more often denote transactions that are permitted. For instance, sales of inventory in the ordinary course of business would be a carve-out to asset sale restrictions.

Change of control A provision that triggers a full repayment of debt upon the change of ownership of or control over the issuer. In the case of bonds, a change of control usually creates a put right where the bondholders can require the issuer to repurchase their bonds at a 1% premium. With leveraged loans, a change of control is usually an event of default that results in the acceleration of the debt.

CLO arbitrage The difference between the yield on the assets less the yield on the liabilities of a CLO. The CLO arbitrage can be thought of as the excess spread that benefits the equity of a CLO.

Collateral leakage This is when important assets included in the collateral that might constitute a downside recovery are distributed to junior claims.

Collateralized Loan Obligations (CLOs) Structured finance vehicles that buy a pool of leveraged loans and finance that purchase with tranches of debt and equity with varying payment priority.

Committed financing See Underwritten offering.

Corporate raiders Financiers that buy large stakes in a corporation and then use shareholder voting rights to exert influence. A corporate raider might seek to take over a company or pressure its board of directors or management team to take actions that will cause its stake to appreciate in value.

Correlation Measures the linear relationship between the directional moves of two data sets and ascribes a value between −1 to 1 depending on the strength of this relationship.

Covenant-lite A term that refers to leveraged loans that lack financial maintenance covenants and therefore only includes incurrence-based covenants similar to high yield bonds.

Covenants Provisions that impose obligations or limitations on the borrower.

Credit agreement A legal contract that outlines the key economic terms, issuer representations, covenants, default provisions, and voting rights that govern a leveraged loan.

Credit spread The difference between the yield and the risk-free rate of a financial debt instrument. The credit spread is also known as the risk premium.

Current return The running rate of return of an investment, calculated by dividing the interest income by the purchase price. If a bond has a 10% interest rate and the bond is bought at a price of 70, it would have a 14.3% current return (10%/ 70% = 14.3%). This concept is also known as effective yield.

Daily liquidity Refers to the ability to redeem capital with one day's notice. Mutual funds offer daily liquidity to investors at the end of the day's net asset value or NAV. This is a statutory requirement of the 1940 Investment Act.

Alternative funds such as hedge funds offer less frequent liquidity, such as monthly, quarterly, or even less frequent.

Debt incurrence   Refers to the ability of the issuer to incur more debt. The debt incurrence negative covenant spells out under what conditions this can be done.

Debut issuer   Refers to an issuer that is accessing the high yield market for the first time.

Default loss   The amount of impairment to a debt issue in the event of a default. If a bond is bought at par or 100% and it is only worth 60% after the company defaults, the default loss would be 40%.

Deferred sales load   A fee that mutual fund investors incur when selling shares often within a certain time period. This is similar to a redemption fee.

Distressed investors   Investors who focus on buying debt claims that are trading at a discount such as under 75%–80% of par or have a high spread of L+1000 or greater. Distressed investors often seek to buy debt issues for companies undergoing or expected to undergo a restructuring.

Downgrade   A negative change in a credit rating. Rating agencies can upgrade or downgrade previously assigned credit ratings based on developments in the reference entity's fundamentals or outlook.

Due diligence   A term that refers to the evaluation process a potential investor undertakes to validate the investment opportunity, understand risks, and confirm all material facts are accurate.

EBITDA   A proxy for the cash flow available to service debt obligations. EBITDA refers to earnings before interest, taxes, depreciation, and amortization.

EBITDA cures   A provision that treats a capital contribution as EBITDA for purposes of testing the financial covenants. EBITDA cures are usually limited in the number of times with which they can be used. The capital contribution allows the company to avoid an event of default on a financial covenant test.

EBITDAR   EBITDAR is a calculation often used with retailers or businesses with significant rental costs. By excluding costs, it's easier to compare a company's operating performance with others in its industry that might have a different mix of owned versus rented properties. See EBITDA.

Effective yield   See Current return.

Enterprise value   Concerns the firm's value and is often referred to as just "EV." When a business is taken private, the enterprise value is the sum of debt and equity capital raised by the company less any balance sheet cash. If a business is public, the enterprise value would be the face value of the debt plus the market capitalization of the stock less any balance sheet cash. Preferred stock and minority interested are also included in the enterprise value calculation. The idea behind enterprise value is to provide an estimate of what a business is worth. This is different than market capitalization, which focuses on just what the equity is worth.

Equity clawback   A provision in bonds that allows an issuer to repay approximately 35%–40% of the bond offering at par plus the coupon with the cash proceeds from an equity offering. When a bond is in its no-call period, the equity clawback provides a means to repay the debt issue without triggering the make-whole premium. This is done so not to dissuade the issuer from raising equity or going public, events which can de-risk the credit profile.

Events of default   Refers to the provisions in credit agreements and indentures that if breached would result in the issuer defaulting under that contract. Events of default usually include failure to make payments on debt, failure to comply with covenants, change of control (in credit agreements), and inaccuracy of representations and warranties.

Excess cash flow sweep   Refers to a credit agreement provision that requires a percentage of an issuer's free cash flow to be directed toward the repayment of debt. Leveraged loans often require issuers to use 50% of their annual free cash flow to repay outstanding borrowings until certain financial criteria are met.

Face amount   The total dollar amount of a debt issue. Also referred to as the notional amount or notional value.

Fallen angels   Investment grade debt that had been downgraded to below investment grade status. The early high yield market consisted primarily of fallen angels.

Financial covenants   See Maintenance covenants.

Financial Industry Regulatory Authority (FINRA)   The largest independent securities regulator in the United States, FINRA regulates over 4,000 member securities firm and exchange markets.

Financial sponsor   A term that refers to the private equity firm that "sponsors" a leveraged buyout or makes a control investment. The track record, reputation, and resources of the financial sponsor are important considerations to lenders of leveraged buyouts. See Private equity firm.

First lien   A leveraged loan issued in the speculative grade debt market in which lenders have senior and the highest priority claim on an issuer's collateral and earnings.

First lien loans   Loans that maintain a priority security interest in the company's collateral, which causes that loan to be senior to most other debt claims. Most leveraged loans are first lien loans.

Fixed rate   Refers to interest payments on a debt instrument that are at a set rate and do not change. Fixed rate debt stands in contrast to floating rate debt.

Flexed   Refers to an increase in the interest rate or other enhancement in terms such as the original issue discount (OID) on a new debt issue to benefit investors. Syndicated offerings are flexed when there is insufficient demand for the offering. This results in less favorable terms to the issuer.

Floating rate   Refers to interest payments that reset periodically based on a spread to an underlying risk-free rate. Leveraged loan interest payments usually reset quarterly based on changes in LIBOR.

Free cash flow   A metric used to assess the amount of cash a business generates annually. In the high yield market, free cash flow is most commonly calculated by taking EBITDA and then subtracting interest expense, taxes, capital expenditures, and changes to working capital.

Fungibility   Additional debt is considered fungible with the previously issued debt if it bears the same CUSIP number. If additional debt is under a different CUSIP number it may not be as liquid as the previous debt issue.

Grower baskets   Baskets that are limited by the greater of a dollar amount or a percentage of total assets (or sometimes percentages of tangible assets or consolidated annual EBITDA).

Guaranteed   Debt that is guaranteed by an operating company essentially has a direct claim on the operating company's assets just as if it resided at that entity. A guarantee is a legal obligation that requires the operating company to use its assets to service that debt.

Hard call   Refers to call protection that offers the issuer limited ability to avoid paying the prepayment penalties should it seek to repay the debt early. This stands in contrast to soft call and is a form of yield enhancement.

High water mark   Ensures a fund manager does not get paid for negative performance and serves as an investor protection. A high water mark requires assets that decline in value to reach their previous peak value before additional performance fees can be paid.

High yield   Debt rated below investment grade or BBB-/Baa3 by major rating agencies such as Moody's Investor Services, Standard & Poor's, or Fitch Ratings.

Holding company (Holdco)   The legal entity that owns the equity of the operating company (or Opco).

Holding company notes   High yield bonds issued at a holding company. These obligations are junior to all operating company claims but senior to the equity.

Hurdle rate   Minimum return that must be achieved which might be 5%–8%.

Idiosyncratic risk   Risk specific to a particular investment. The idiosyncratic risk of a debt issue is firm-specific risk that is uncorrelated to the overall market.

Illiquidity risk   The inability to sell holdings in the secondary market without a substantial loss in value.

Impaired   When a debt claim receives less value than the amount of principal outstanding.

Incentive fee   See Carry fee.

Incurrence-based covenants A type of covenant that is only tested when an action is taken. Usually, compliance with a test such as an interest coverage ratio is required for the action to be taken. The goal of incurrence-based covenants is not to entirely impede business flexibility but to ensure debt claims have sufficient coverage post any transaction that is potentially value detracting.

Indenture A legal contract that outlines the key economic terms, issuer representations, covenants, default provisions, and voting rights that govern a high yield bond.

Index hugger An investment vehicle that implements a passive strategy by replicating an index or benchmark. Index huggers operate with low fees and seek to minimize tracking error.

Interest coverage ratio A metric that conveys how well an issuer's cash flow covers its interest expense. The interest coverage ratio is defined as interest expense divided by EBITDA.

Investment banks Financial institutions such as J.P. Morgan, Barclays, Bank of America Merrill Lynch, Citigroup, Goldman Sachs, and Morgan Stanley that serve as important financial intermediaries between issuers and investors. Investment banks facilitate a wide range of transactions including mergers and acquisitions, IPOs, and capital raises. For high yield issuers, investment banks provide capital markets advice, use their balance sheets to provide committed capital, raise high yield bonds and leveraged loans, and make secondary markets following the primary issuance. Investment banks also provide many buyers of high yield debt with financing.

Investment grade Debt rated Baa1/BBB+ and above by major rating agencies such as Moody's Investor Services, Standard & Poor's, or Fitch Ratings.

Junk bonds A term used to describe high yield debt during the market's early years, when high yield consisted primarily of fallen angels, or investment grade debt that had been downgraded to "junk" status. Over time, below investment grade debt became more commonly referred to as "high yield."

Know-your-customer (KYC) A standard process where the identity of an entity is verified to ensure legal compliance.

Layering Refers to the incurrence of debt that would rank senior to the debt purported to be protected by the covenants. Layering is also referred to as priming.

Leverage ratio A ratio that conveys the quantum of debt as a multiple of the issuer's cash flow. The leverage ratio is defined as total debt divided by EBITDA.

Leverage Another word for debt or borrowed money. Leverage is used in buyouts to enhance the potential return of equity investments.

Leveraged buyout (LBO) A type of transaction where a company or asset is purchased through a combination of equity and debt borrowings. LBOs are commonly employed by financial sponsors who use the target company's assets and cash flows as collateral to raise debt that helps fund a significant portion of the purchase price.

Leveraged recapitalization   Also called a "leveraged recap," it refers to a type of high yield transaction where debt capital is raised to fund a share repurchase or distribution to owners. Leveraged recapitalizations result in the company having more debt or leverage and the equity holders either obtaining a return or having less "skin in the game." This type of transaction usually occurs in situations where the underlying credit has performed and lenders are willing to lend more capital, because they believe the risk-reward is attractive, even if that capital provides no economic benefit to the enterprise.

LIBOR floor   A minimum level of the LIBOR component of the interest rate. Due to the zero interest rate policy (ZIRP) implemented by the Federal Reserve in 2008, high yield market markers established LIBOR floors to provide a minimum rate for LIBOR, which is most often set at 100 bps or 1.0%.

Lien subordination   Lien subordination occurs with secured claims and refers to one lien being subordinated or explicitly junior to another lien. Second lien loans have liens that are subordinated to first lien loans for example.

London Interbank Offered Rate (LIBOR)   An interest rate that some of the world's leading banks charge each other for short-term loans. LIBOR is a benchmark interest rate calculated for five different currencies (US$, EUR, GBP, JPY, CHF). In the high yield market, LIBOR sets the base rate for which most leveraged loans are priced at a spread to.

Maintenance covenants   An ongoing obligation for an issuer to demonstrate its financial health. Maintenance covenants are tested quarterly and often require an issuer to be in compliance with a total leverage and interest coverage ratio. Maintenance covenants are absent in almost all bond indentures. Failure to meet a maintenance covenant constitutes an event of default. Maintenance covenants are also referred to as financial covenants.

Make-whole premium   A feature related to call protection that reflects the penalty an issuer must pay in order to repay non-callable debt. If a bond is non-callable for five years and an issuer wants to repay the bond in year two, it would have to pay a make-whole premium in addition to the notional amount of the bond. The make-whole premium would equal the present value of all payments due through the first call date, including coupons and the pre-payment premium, discounted at a rate generally equal to T+50bps with "T" representing the rate of treasury debt with a comparable maturity. Make-whole premiums are usually very expensive to issuers.

Management roadshow   During the process of raising capital from investors, the management team of a company travels around the country and even overseas to meet with potential investors. This process allows investors to meet management and ask questions directly.

Mandatory amortization A set notional amount that must be paid periodically. Leveraged loans often have a requirement for issuers to repay 1% of the total notional amount per year.

Margin finance Involves depositing collateral with a broker to secure low-cost borrowings to buy stocks, bonds, and options. The borrowings provide the potential to enhance capital returns on the investment.

Margin of safety For stock pickers, value investing refers to buying a stock at a price below its intrinsic value. For debt investors, the margin of safety typically refers to the amount the enterprise value could decline before debt claims became impaired.

Marked-to-market Valuing an asset or portfolio at market prices. This is often done to establish collateral or net asset value.

Maturity wall A point in the near future where a substantial amount of high yield debt becomes due.

Mergers and Acquisitions (M&A) Involves buying, selling, or combining different companies. The end result of a merger or acquisition are practically the same, but there are technical differences to the terms. A merger is when the two companies combine to create a new company and the old companies cease to exist, which is what happened when Daimler Benz and Chrysler combined to form DaimlerChrysler. An acquisition is when one company is bought out by another.

Most Favored Nation (MFN) clause Appearing in leveraged loans, the MFN clause provides that, to the extent new debt carries yield that exceeds the yield on the original tranche by more than a certain cushion, usually 25–50 bps, the yield on the original tranche is increased to maintain the same cushion.

Negative covenants Provisions that impose restrictions on corporate actions that can adversely affect collateral that support a debt claim. Negative covenants govern actions including asset sales, the incurrence of additional debt, distributions to shareholders, and the incurrence of liens.

Net Asset Value (NAV) The market value of all assets less liabilities and then dividing this amount by the number of issued shares.

Net leverage ratio Similar to the leverage ratio but subtracts cash from total debt before dividing by EBITDA. See Leverage ratio.

New issue forward calendar A list of all high yield new issues in the market or expected to be sold. The new issue calendar provides an estimate of high yield supply.

Notional amount or notional value The total dollar amount of a debt issue. Also referred to as the face amount.

Odd lots In the equity markets, odd lots refer to trades of less than 100 shares. In the high yield market, odd lots are more commonly thought of as trades of less than $1 million.

Offer   Also known as "ask." Refers to the price at which a security or other financial instrument can be sold (e.g. the offer price).

Offering memorandum   Also referred to as an "OM," this serves as a legal document that provides buyers with important information related to the debt offering including the transaction structure, credit highlights, business and financial profile, and legal terms.

Operating company (Opco)   The legal entity that is guaranteed by, and owns the equity of, operating subsidiaries.

Original Issue Discount (OID)   The discount from par at which a loan or bond is offered for sale to investors. If a loan is issued at 99, the OID is 100 bps, 1 point, or 1%.

OTC market   See Over-the-counter market.

Over-subscribed   A new debt offering raised in the primary market that receives more financial commitments than the amount of capital intended to be raised. In most cases, the investment bank or arranger will decrease the spread or interest rate, in order to take advantage of favorable market conditions and offset excess demand for the loan.

Over-the-counter market   Refers to the trading of securities, loans, and other financial instruments through a network of trading relationships rather than a public exchange, like the NYSE or NASDAQ. OTC markets are decentralized without a physical infrastructure and are less regulated than national exchanges. Most high yield debt trades OTC.

Par   The face value of a stock or other security. Par equals a price of 100.

Pari passu   A term meaning equivalent. Debt obligations that are *pari passu* have the same ranking or legal status as it relates to payment priority.

Payment blockage notice   A notice senior noteholders give to subordinated noteholders that prevents the subordinated noteholders from receiving interest payments. This is done to limit the amount of cash being distributed to junior claims, which might otherwise constitute important recovery to more senior claim holders.

Payment default   A monetary default such as when an issuer misses an interest or principal payment.

Payment subordination   Most relevant to senior subordinated notes, refers to debt whose interest payments can be blocked by more senior claims.

Payment-In-Kind (PIK)   Debt whose interest can be paid by issuing additional debt claims rather than paying cash.

Permitted acquisitions   Describes the ability of the issuer to grow by buying additional businesses. Oftentimes, the amount of acquisitions that can be made and financed with debt capital is capped and subject to a basket or ratio test.

PIK toggle   A feature in certain bonds that allow the issuer to pay a lower interest rate in cash or a higher interest rate in additional debt.

Prepayments   Refers to debt repayments prior to the maturity of the instrument.

Price   The value of a debt instrument stated as a percentage of its notional amount. A high yield bond or leveraged loan can trade above or below a price of 100. Note, the percentage sign is omitted when stating high yield prices.

Primary market   The market where issuers obtain funds through the sale of new securities, loans, and other instruments. Also referred to as the new issue market, the primary market stands in contrast to the secondary market where existing securities and assets are traded between investors.

Prime brokerage   A service provided by investment banks to primarily hedge funds. Prime brokerage involves providing financing for investments and securities borrowing for short selling among other things. Many prime brokerage businesses also include a service called capital introductions or "cap intro." The capital introductions team helps hedge funds meet prospective investors.

Priming   See Layering.

Private equity firm   An investment firm that pools capital from institutions, pension funds, endowments, high net worth individuals, and other investors to make equity investments that provide control or influence over companies. Often called financial sponsors, these firms' equity investments are not in publicly listed stock and therefore are called private equity. Private equity firms pursue leveraged buyouts, venture capital, and growth capital investments.

Private placements   Privately negotiated transactions with more sophisticated investors. Private placements differ from public offerings in that interest in the transaction is not solicited more broadly. In a private placement, the issuer works with one or a few parties to raise capital which then rarely trades in the secondary market.

Project financings   A type of high yield transaction in which an issuer raises debt in order to back a business expansion, for example, a new casino construction, factory equipment, or utility infrastructure. The debt raised in project financings primarily relies on the project's assets and projected cash flows for debt service. Sometimes parent guarantees are provided which can reduce the risk associated with new ventures and therefore lower the cost of the debt capital being raised.

Prospectus   A type of offering memorandum for high yield bonds, which is required by and filed with the Securities and Exchange Commission. See Offering memorandum.

Qualified Institutional Buyer (QIB)   A purchaser of securities that is deemed to be financially sophisticated and can participate in less regulated markets and financial instruments. Rule 144A requires an institution to have $100 million of securities among other requirements.

Ranking   A legal term that denotes a debt's status or where a claim stands in relations to others. Rank distinctions are made on (1) whether or not the debt is secured and (2) its level of seniority.

Ratings arbitrage   Refers to a difference in the returns of two debt instruments with the same rating. For example, a AAA rated commercial mortgage back security could have a credit spread of 125 bps, compared to a AAA CLO liability spread of 150 bps. The 25 bps of excess spread provided by the AAA CLO liability is considered the ratings arbitrage.

Ratio debt   Describes a debt basket that is not limited by a dollar amount but rather is subject to a certain financial ratio, most commonly an interest coverage ratio in bond indentures or a leverage ratio in credit agreements.

Recovery rates or recoveries   Terms that represent the principal value of a debt claim remaining post default, expressed as a percentage of face value.

Refinancing   A high yield transaction where existing debt is repaid with new borrowings. This is typically done to lower the company's cost of borrowings or to extend a maturity.

Relative value   An assessment of the risk, liquidity or return of one security, loan or asset class versus another. Relative value investors can invest broadly to find the best perceived risk-return.

Remedies block   Following an event of default, a remedies block prevents junior debtholders from accelerating their debt for a certain period of time ranging from 90 days to 180 days, unless the senior debt has been accelerated first. This is also known as a standstill.

Restricted payments   Refers to payments that essentially represent collateral leakage and are therefore restricted. This can include distributions to the equity holders and prepayments of junior debt.

Restricted subsidiary   A subsidiary that is subject to covenants. Not every restricted subsidiary is a guarantor of the debt. The distinction is important in downside scenarios as other more junior claims may have a pari passu interest in non-guarantor restricted subsidiaries.

Reverse-flexed   Refers to a decrease in the interest rate or other modifications that result in less beneficial terms to investors or more favorable terms to the issuer. Reverse-flex occurs when the amount of investor interest in a debt offering significantly exceeds the amount being offered.

Revolving credit facility   A capital line that provides the issuer with the flexibility to draw-down and repay capital based on its needs.

Risk-free rate   The rate at which the government can borrow. High yield issuers pay more than the risk-free rate for borrowings in order to compensate investors for the possibility of loss. Risk-free rates therefore set a floor on corporate borrowing costs.

Risk premium   See Credit spread.

Rollover   When an investor decides to maintain its investment in an issuer that is refinancing its debt, it is considered to be "rolling over" its interest. Essentially it means that the investor will get repaid on its existing holdings and then will reinvest in the new financing.

Rule 144A   Exempts issuers from publicly filing financial statements with the Securities and Exchange Commission provided that the securities are sold to qualified institutional buyers (QIBS), which generally are large institutional investors that own at least $100 million in securities. Under Rule 144A, QIBs can freely trade with each other, which has enhanced the liquidity of these unregistered offerings. Many high yield bonds are sold pursuant to Rule 144A.

Sacred rights   Actions that, by law, cannot be taken without unanimous consent. The four sacred rights are: reducing interest rates, extending the maturity, releasing liens, and reducing the amount of loans.

Seasoned issuer   A company that has outstanding high yield debt and therefore has an investor following.

Second lien loans   Loans that maintain a security interest in the company's collateral but that lien is subordinated to the lien held by the first lien term loan.

Secondary market   The market for existing securities, assets, and other financial instruments. In contrast to the primary market, the secondary market is where investors transact with each other rather than the originating entity.

Secured   Refers to debt that has a lien on, or security interest in, assets that constitute collateral pledged in support of its claim.

Securities borrowing   In order for a security to be sold short, the security must be borrowed. Investment banks lend securities to short sellers and charge a fee for the service in addition to requiring collateral to be posted and maintained. The security is delivered back to the investment bank when the short is covered and the security repurchased.

Senior secured notes   Refers to bonds that have a lien on assets. Senior secured notes typically have a first lien on certain collateral and a second lien on more liquid collateral (that might be secured by an asset based facility to provide the company with a working capital line).

Senior secured   Debt that benefits from liens on assets and payment seniority over other debt claims.

Senior subordinated notes   High yield bonds typically issued at the operating company that are junior in right of payment to any first and second lien loans as well as to senior notes.

Seniority   A descriptive term often included in the name of an instrument itself and relates to an ordering of payments for claims with similar collateral. If a company has two bonds outstanding, one might be called "senior notes" while the other is called "junior notes." Senior claims, as the terms suggests, get repaid prior to junior claims.

Sharpe ratio   A standard performance metric calculated by taking the annualized total return of a risky asset in excess of the risk-free rate and then dividing this amount by the volatility or standard deviation of returns.

Soft call   Refers to call protection that only applies if the issuer seeks to refinance the loan with lower yielding debt. A soft call is a form of yield protection.

Speculative grade   A term used by rating agencies that refers to debt rated below BBB-/Baa3. Speculative grade, below investment grade, and high yield are all terms used interchangeably.

Standstill   See Remedies block.

Structural subordination   Refers to debt that is junior because it resides at a more remote holding company.

Subordination   A legal term that describes the interrelationship, or relative priority, among various tranches of debt. High yield has three types of subordination: (1) payment subordination, (2) lien subordination, and (3) structural subordination.

Technical default   A non-monetary default such as a covenant breach.

Total return   The actual return of an investment or asset class over a specified time period. The total return of high yield is derived from interest income, fees, prepayment premiums, price appreciation/depreciation, and realized gains/losses.

Total Return Swap (TRS)   A swap transaction where an investment grade bank uses its low-cost capital to buy higher yielding assets for a client such as leveraged loans. The client posts collateral in an agreed-upon amount to protect the bank from losses. The bank charges a fee on the notional amount of assets purchased and the client benefits from all residual income. A TRS can provide financial leverage for assets that are not securities and therefore ineligible for margin finance.

TRACE (Trade Reporting and Compliance Engine)   Developed by FINRA in 2002 to facilitate the mandatory reporting of OTC secondary market transactions in eligible fixed income securities. All broker/dealers who are FINRA member firms have an obligation to report transactions in corporate bonds to TRACE under an SEC approved set of rules.

Tracking error   A measure of how closely a portfolio follows the index to which it is benchmarked. This is often assessed by returns or standard deviation differences.

Transferability   Refers to the ability to transfer interests in a leveraged loan. Leveraged loans are transferable, or more precisely "assignable," usually with the consent of the issuer and the administrative agent of the loan facility.

Under-subscribed   When a primary market offering receives less investor commitments than the amount of capital intended to be raised it is considered under-subscribed. If an offering is under-subscribed, the lead investment bank, working in connection with the company's owners, will usually increase the interest rate or provide other more favorable terms to investors in order to garner more interest in the transaction.

Underwrite   A term that refers to taking balance sheet risk. When an investment bank underwrites a high yield offering, it takes the risk of that offering not selling to investors and remaining on its balance sheet.

Underwritten offering   Refers to a transaction where an investment bank guarantees to provide capital to support a transaction such as a leveraged buyout or acquisition. Investment banks must underwrite debt offerings, or commit to be a lender of last resort, in order for certain deals to proceed. Underwritten commitments, also referred to as committed financings, are usually intended to be sold to investors.

Unitranche   A type of loan popular with small to mid-sized companies. In this type of financing, a lender provides one loan that encompasses both the senior and junior debt risk instead of parsing it up.

Unrestricted subsidiary   A subsidiary that is not subject to the covenants and is free to operate without regard to the restrictions imposed by the high yield documentation.

Unsecured   Refers to debt that does not have a lien on any assets. Unsecured debt stands in contrast to secured debt.

Upgrade   A positive change in a credit rating. Rating agencies can upgrade or downgrade previously assigned credit ratings based on developments in the reference entity's fundamentals or outlook.

Volatility   A measure of risk that is based on total return deviations from a mean return.

WARF score   The Weighted Average Rating Factor score. WARF is a measure used to determine the credit quality of a portfolio.

Warrants   A security that gives the holder the right to buy equity shares within a certain time frame at an exercise price. Early mezzanine financings sometimes came with "penny warrants" to provide additional compensation for the risk.

Yield   The rate of return on a debt instrument based on the price of the debt, interest rate, and other economic features.

Yield curve   A line that plots the interest rates of comparable quality debt but with differing maturity dates. The yield curve most commonly refers to the interest rates of the 3-month, 2-year, 5-year and 30-year U.S. Treasury debt.

Yield-to-call   The rate of return an investor would realize if a bond is called by the issuer at the first call date.

Yield-to-maturity   The rate of return an investor would realize if a bond is repaid at maturity.

Yield-to-worst   The lowest rate of return that can be received on a bond based on the issuer's call schedule. For investors, it is the worst possible yield scenario barring principal loss.

Index

Compiled by INDEXING SPECIALISTS (UK) Ltd., Indexing House, 306A Portland Road, Hove, East Sussex BN3 5LP United Kingdom.